TOKYO STORY

STEVE WIDE &
MICHELLE MACKINTOSH

Hardie Grant
EXPLORE

いか焼
アサヒビール

WRITE YOURSELF INTO TOKYO'S STORY
東京の物語をあなた自身のストーリーに

Konnichiwa!

The 1953 Yasujirô Ozu film *Tokyo Story*, is one of our favourite pieces of cinema. One of its central themes, contrasting old-world Tokyo with rapidly approaching modernity, rings true for us as this can still be seen in the city today. Our own Tokyo Story was pencilled in on our first (honeymoon) trip and now, 65 trips later, we have added new chapters with each visit, and our story is still unfolding.

Tokyo is a vast city, which may seem overwhelming at first, but when you start to look closer, you'll uncover a network of smaller neighbourhoods, each with their own unique culture and atmosphere. You'll discover it's a city with people that care about small daily tasks and place importance in creativity. Getting to know these Tokyo moments is the key to understanding the city's detailed and engrossing plot.

To be a protagonist in the story of this magnificent city has been a life highlight for us and this book shares those memorable and perfect moments through listings which, for us, reveal the intricate layers of Tokyo. Join us to uncover future fashions, the best ramen and matcha, ultra-cool listening bars, vibrant pop culture, vintage stores, retro cafes, world-class museums, unique architecture, and beautiful green spaces. Then there are the hidden enclaves that still have traces of classic Edo (the original name for Tokyo) traditions. You'll also find handy advice on navigating Tokyo's many plot twists, including train stations (some are as big as city blocks).

Once you get your bearings, your own Tokyo Story will begin to unfold and the colourful characters and moments of intrigue will reveal themselves. Turn left rather than right, peer down side streets and use all of your senses to make the most of every moment (and season).

There is no other place in the world like Tokyo, so let your story begin.

Steve Wide and Michelle Mackintosh

TOKYO NEIGHBOURHOODS

Tokyo's many neighbourhoods can give this large city an almost village-y feel, with each area proudly cultivating its own atmosphere, history and specialties. Shopping precincts sit happily next door to traditional pockets; you may find yourself going from high-tech to lo-fi all in a matter of hours. Understanding how the neighbourhoods are placed, and how they are linked, will have you Tokyo travel-ready in no time.

AKIHABARA
秋葉原

‣ Akihabara is near Ueno, Ryogoku, Nihombashi and the Imperial Palace.

Looking for that rare giant robot or Sailor Moon collectible? Akiba (as it is affectionately known by Tokyo locals) is a multiverse for tech junkies and obsessive fans of anime and manga. If figurines, computers and vintage toys are your bag, you've made it to the top level. Pulsating Chuo-dori (streets are called 'dori') is a riot of flashing lights, blaring music and bleeps and bloops pinging from pop-coloured buildings, where you'll lose hours leafing through the latest graphic novel or pretending not to play with various vintage or new-release toys (they're not toys, they're collectibles). It's gaming heaven, IRL. Also, it's not nicknamed Electric Town for nothing. Here, you can glimpse the future in electronics and score the latest new-fangled gadgets by heading to the megastores on the main streets or trawling through smaller, rambling treasure troves that populate a labyrinth of alleys and lanes around Akihabara station. Coffee shops sell bottomless cups and character-themed pastries to keep you wired all day. Chances are if you put on your adult-sized Astro Boy outfit and go for a stroll, no one will bat an eyelid.

AOYAMA
青山

‣ Aoyama is near Omotesando-dori, Harajuku, Shibuya, Roppongi and Nezu Museum.

Aoyama is a neighbourhood of contrasts. At one end of Omotesando-dori, mad crowds gather in the teen magnet of Harajuku. However, Aoyama at the other end of the broad avenue gives way to chic, understated Tokyo style. Once an Edo period (1603–1867) samurai playground, there is an atmosphere of calm in Aoyama's leafy streets and tiny lanes, lined with fashion boutiques, florists, organic cafes and handmade goods stores. In-the-know, style-savvy shoppers come here to update their wardrobe or select that perfect artisan ceramic to level up their home. People watching is an inspiration in Aoyama and you'll always see someone who has distilled their sartorial essence into the pinnacle of street style and turned the Aoyama streets into their own breezy catwalk. Issey Miyake and COMME des GARÇONS command much of the real estate and many of the stores have art projects and installations in shopfront windows, making them look more like galleries than retail outlets. Coveted Japanese and European fashion labels are housed in famous architectural buildings, brave new additions to a landscape that once featured temples, shrines and samurai houses. At the end of Omotesando-dori, the Nezu Museum sits serenely, known for its stunning gardens, atmospheric gallery and teahouses.

ASAKUSA
浅草

Asakusa's temples, shrines and time-worn streets form an impressive glimpse into the beauty of old Japan and a festive atmosphere hints at the area's past as an entertainment district. It's all those things for sure, but get off the main streets and you'll be walking along authentic lantern-filled side streets with local sentos (public, regular water baths), potted gardens, twelfth-generation broom-makers and long-standing stores and street stalls. Tiny shrines peek out from between ramshackle shops and even Asakusa station pays homage to the area's Buddhist heritage with a red shrine facsimile constructed over the Ginza line entrance. Ready your camera as photo opportunities are everywhere, from majestic Senso-ji temple to colourful Nakamise Shopping Street. Philippe Starck's Asahi Super Dry Beer Hall with its famous 'Golden Turd' architecture gives a sly wink to fellow futurist the Skytree, a monumental tower with jaw-dropping views of the city's expanse. Nearby Kappabashi-dori is a kilometres-long shopping street selling kitchenwear.

‣ Asakusa is near Kuramae, Ueno, Kappabashi-dori and the Skytree.

DAIKANYAMA
代官山

The chic-yet-understated boutiques scattered around the lazy backstreets of Daikanyama bring an air of luxe to this quiet neighbourhood, however the influx of young Tokyo-ites on weekends make sure that there's also a definite street-level appeal. Daikanyama is the home of revered Tokyo designers, vintage emporiums, craft stores and indie galleries. Meet your friends under the large green flower near the station for a lazy day punctuated by shopping, marvelling at Tokyo's clever residential architecture and spending some quality time leafing through the plethora of latest-release books at Tsutaya's architecturally designed emporium T-Site, before lounging the afternoon away sipping superb cafe lattes in one of the fashionable Western-style cafes.

‣ Daikanyama is near Nakameguro, Ebisu and Shibuya.

EBISU
恵比寿

‣ Ebisu is near Daikanyama, Nakameguro, Meguro and Shibuya.

Shopping and business district by day, the real Ebisu gets out of bed, puts on its engineered jeans and opens a beer before heading out for the night. Roller doors pull up to unveil tiny bars, eateries and night cafes that get crowded and loud very quickly. A lot of the fun here is rubbing shoulders with salarymen who have hopped off the train for a quick ramen, or hip young Tokyo-ites out for a night on the tiles at one of Ebisu's many bars. It's a city divided. On one side the commercial business district hides a cutting-edge photography museum, TOP, the Tokyo Photographic Art Museum, and some sky-high dining with astounding views at Yebisu Garden Place. Around the station however, the streets are crammed with izakaya (pubs with small plate food) and small maker stores. The beer is good here of course, Ebisu is the home of Yebisu beer, one of the world's best, and namesake brand Evisu jeans are also made here, the perfect metaphor for a neighbourhood that is quirky, inventive and laid-back.

GAKUGEIDAIGAKU
学芸大学

‣ Gakugeidaigaku is near Jiyugaoka, Nakameguro and Meguro.

A quick ride from Shibuya station, tucked between Nakameguro and Jiyugaoka stations is one of our favourite local areas. Gakugeidaigaku has much more of a residential neighbourhood feel compared to next-door Meguro. There are plenty of quaint eateries, long-standing hole-in-the-wall street food outlets and some great shopping finds amongst the patchwork of tiny streets, most of which are lamp-lined and soundtracked by piped music, lending the area a gentle yet festive atmosphere. Gakudai (as the locals call it) is perfect for the new coffee houses, craft beer joints and doughnut shops that are springing up among the Western-style cafes and non-Japanese Asian eateries, bookstores and craft and homewares stores. This the perfect place for a weekend stroll, leafing through vintage magazines or munching on a handmade onigiri (rice ball) before you head towards nearby Jiyugaoka.

GINZA
銀座

‣ Ginza is near Tokyo Station, Marunouchi, Yurakucho, Nihombashi and Tsukiji Market.

Built on a swamp and burnt almost to the ground in 1872, this opulent precinct has risen like a phoenix from the ashes. Reinventing itself as the site of the silver mint since 1612, and a banking district over 100 years ago, Ginza is Tokyo at its grandest. Home to some of the world's oldest and most luxurious department stores, it's the best place to glimpse kimono-clad ladies shopping in fashion boutiques and lunching in Michelin-star restaurants. Classic Japanese paper, fabric and incense shops and established tempura houses are dotted among the flashy new flagship stores of Japanese staples like Uniqlo, Loft and Muji. Luxe European brands peacock along the thoroughfares (check out the eye-popping Louis Vuitton, Pola, Mikimoto and Ginza Place buildings). The classic Kabuki-za theatre and nearby Tsukiji Outer Market give Ginza a real sense of history. Don't mind the iconic Wako clock keeping time; stick around as day turns to night to see one of Tokyo's quintessential neon landscapes. To add to the allure, on the weekends Ginza becomes 'pedestrian heaven' between 12pm and 5pm, when Chuo-dori is closed to traffic.

HARAJUKU
原宿

‣ Harajuku is near Yoyogi, Shibuya, Shinjuku, Aoyama, the Meiji shrine, Yoyogi park and Omotesando-dori.

Boasting a network of seriously fabulous backstreets, Harajuku holds the key to some of Tokyo's unmissable shopping, dining and people-watching experiences. Despite its extensive Edo history and the presiding presence of the Meiji shrine, energetic Harajuku has reinvented itself since the 1920s as a youth destination with a vengeance. The mad crush of Takeshita-dori and the majestic sweep of Omotesando-dori are iconic Tokyo destinations and if you are looking for thronging crowds and pulsating energy, you've come to the right place. The thrilling days of the '90s when the eyes of the fashion world were trained on Harajuku, and Belle and Sebastian and Gwen Stefani name-checked it in their songs are long over, but young Tokyo-ites still comes here to flaunt eye-popping fashion and queue for hours at the newest fluffy pancake or decorative sweets cafe. Omotesando-dori's wide tree-lined street is reminiscent of a French boulevard where international brands vie for attention and showcase beautifully curated fashion in spectacular, contemporary buildings crafted by a who's who of Japanese architecture.

JIYUGAOKA & KUHONBUTSU
自由が丘&九品仏

‣ Jiyugaoka and Kuhonbutsu are near Gakugeidaigaku, Ebisu and Nakameguro.

Ah, lazy, breezy Jiyugaoka! Around 10min from Shibuya on an express train, this relaxing precinct will make you feel like you've left the madness of the city far behind. Most shops go with a French theme here; you won't be out of place if you hit Marie Claire-dori (it's really called that) in a beret and Breton shirt pushing a stroller with a French bulldog peeping out of it. There's a plethora of homewares stores, hand-craft shops, and cafes visited by 30-somethings who seem to be on a permanent go-slow. It's the quintessential Sunday town, so grab a date and spend an afternoon visiting Today's Special, Bake the Shop, Jiyugaoka Sando, Momo Natural and Quatre Saisons Tokio, Moonstar, Popeye and Katakana. Note that if you follow the train line from Jiyugaoka to Kuhonbutsu, you can make a detour towards one of Tokyo's best-kept secrets, Joshin-ji temple, which dates back to 1678. Not far from here is D&Department's cafe-meets-design store, where you can while away a few happy hours.

KICHIJOJI
吉祥寺

‣ Kichijoji is near Nishi-Ogikubo, Koenji and Inokashira park.

Perched on the edge of Inokashira park, this residential neighbourhood is the perfect antidote to the madness of the big city and only 20min away from Shibuya by train on the Inokashira line (make sure you take the express). Ride a bicycle down Nakamichi-dori to check out the independent handmade clothing and design stores. Have dinner and drinks in the tiny bars and eateries of the charming, old-world Harmonica Yokocho alleyway, or stroll down the covered lanes of Sun Road Arcade to shop for food and homewares. A picnic in Inokashira park in cherry blossom season sets the scene for a perfect day. Cruise the lake in the swan boats or stop off at the nearby Ghibli Museum and disappear into Miyazaki's wondrous world of animation. Kichijoji has always been an 'in-the-know' slice of authentic neighbourhood Tokyo, and in a world where knowledge is at everyone's fingertips, it still retains this feeling of a Tokyo secret escape.

KITASANDO
北参道

› Kitasando is near Harajuku, Yoyogi, Sendagaya, Shinjuku and the Meiji-Jingu shrine.

This enclave, wedged between Shibuya and Shinjuku, is a strollable network of streets featuring off-the-radar local cafes and a palpable food culture, as well as small makers and independent clothing stores. Stop by CIBI Corner Store or Kitasando coffee for a pick-me-up on your way to Hatonomori Hachiman shrine, or head north-west to float through the Kitasando torii gate which leads to the Meiji shrine's lesser-known entrance. Hatonomori Hachiman shrine is a Shinto shrine dating to 1789, which features 'mini-Fuji,' a small mountain with a path that emulates the Fuji climbing trail. The shrine is also known for a mass planting of hydrangeas that are vibrant in summer, and irises that are in full bloom in June. The National Noh Theatre is just north of the shrine. Close by is Marc Newson's Urasando public toilet, part of The Tokyo Toilet Project.

KOENJI
高円寺

‣ Koenji is near Ogikubo, Nishi-Ogikubo, Kichijoji and Shinjuku.

Largely unaffected by World War II bombing and the 1980s' construction frenzy, Koenji has the charming look and feel of pre-boom Japan. Its relaxed atmosphere hides a swirling pop culture undercurrent, where late night bars and 'live houses' generate an eclectic music scene. A mecca for mid-century vintage and pre-loved fashion, toys, music and books, there are more than 70 second-hand stores on Koenji's criss-cross network of streets, making it a great place to spend the day browsing – flicking lazily through over-stuffed racks and fossicking in crammed boxes and on teetering shelves. Some of the city's most unique cafes languish in the side streets, up steep stairs and down narrow laneways. Ramen and yakitori joints bubble vibrantly around Koenji station, perfect stops for a refuel and a wee tipple before rolling into a live bar to listen to some of Tokyo's most inventive musicians playing up a storm.

KURAMAE
蔵前

Kuramae is a treasured local neighbourhood, hidden in plain sight. Just a short stroll from busy Asakusa and the sprawling Senso-ji temple, you'll find a more relaxed, low-rise precinct where Mom and Pop stores and famed traditional businesses sit side by side with contemporary cafes, bars and eateries. Mostly though, you'll find the area gets its creative nuance from the many craft and homewares shops. Check store times if you're planning a visit, as a lot of things can be closed on Sundays for example, and you might find that people in this area rise a little later than in the rest of Tokyo. It's the perfect local go-to with a handmade aesthetic that gives it a distinct Tokyo undercurrent.

‣ Kuramae is near Asakusa, Akihabara, Yanesen, Ueno and Kappabashi-dori.

MEGURO
目黒

› Meguro is near Nakameguro, Daikanyama, Shirokanedai and Ebisu.

Sweeping Meguro-dori links two creative neighbourhoods. To the north-east of the station, you'll find a busy area highlighting parks, gardens, teahouses and in-the-know shopping. The east is home to Meguro Sky Garden, a bold and unique eco paradise atop an expressway junction. West of the station you will find a covered arcade crammed with pocket-sized eateries loaded with character and old-world charm. New bars and coffee houses can be found around the river as well as the oft-overlooked but excellent Meguro Museum of Art. In fact, Meguro is an area that often doesn't make it on to people's Tokyo agenda, but hidden amongst the leafy stretches and broad streets are some vibrant Tokyo hubs. After a day exploring the area, walk north from Meguro along the Meguro River canal to arrive just in time for dinner in cosy Nakameguro. This is also a popular sakura (cherry blossom) promenade in spring.

NAKAMEGURO
中目黒

› Nakameguro is near Ebisu, Daikanyama, Shibuya and Meguro.

A target of World War II bombings, ghosts of the past may haunt Nakameguro's central canal, but this low-rise bohemian precinct has reinvented itself as an intimate neighbourhood beloved by Tokyo-ites and sought out by those wanting to get a feel for local Tokyo. Nakameguro has long been making a name for itself as a go-to place for stylish shopping, revamped vintage and cosy cafes and restaurants. The canal is the focal point, fringed with a plethora of choices for food, drink and shopping and, of course, promenading. Over 800 cherry blossom trees line the canal, making it one of the city's best viewing spots during hanami (cherry blossom season). The canopy of thick pink is a sight to behold whether seen from one of the canals' bridges or from the station on its elevated tracks. You can also find out more about cherry blossoms by visiting the nearby Sato Sakura Museum. Much-hyped pizza joints, tiny eateries and coffee hubs call Nakameguro home, thriving in side streets and around the station. Walking from Ebisu to Nakameguro and then to Daikanyama (do this in any order) is one of Tokyo's perfect weekend strolls.

NIPPORI & KITASENJU
日暮里&北千住

‣ Nippori and Kitasenju are near Yanesen, Ueno and Asakusa.

Nippori is a well-established historic town with echoes of old Tokyo. Affectionately known as Fabric Town, warehouses and tiny stores spill out onto the streets with all manner of unique textiles and sewing materials. Wander the back streets visiting small Edo-period (1603–1867) shrines and temples, stopping for a soak in the refurbished historic bathhouse Saito-yu. A hub station of sorts, Nippori serves local JR lines including the Yamanote loop line and the Keisei Skyliner bound for Narita Airport. From Nippori, jump on the Joban line for an 8min ride towards Kitasenju where you'll float into a clutch of small eateries, yakitori joints, bustling izakaya (pubs with small plate food), small makers' stores, local sentos and cafes and dessert houses. Kitasenju is a good spot to blend in with locals and see Japan going about its daily life.

ROPPONGI & AZABUJUBAN
六本木&麻布十番

‣ Roppongi and Azabujuban are near Shibuya, Ebisu and Tokyo Tower.

Roppongi has long held the crown as the go-to precinct to party all night and catch the last train home. Chaotic and noisy, with looming overpasses and streets so wide you can't see the other side, Roppongi's seedy reputation was hard earnt and well deserved. However, this area has undergone a renaissance in recent years with the emergence of the Art Triangle which features some of the world's finest galleries and architecture, and chic shopping mecca Tokyo Midtown. Both have conspired to make Roppongi a must on many tourists' to-do lists. Next-door neighbour Azabujuban is more sedate, with a village-like atmosphere, cobbled streets, traditional shops and family businesses. Azabudai Hills, a mega shopping destination, self-proclaimed green zone and art monolith has sprouted in the middle of Azabu, permanently changing the skyline. Here you'll find the new face of Tokyo; upscale eateries, workstations, fashion and design stores and the popular, immersive teamLab Borderless Digital Art Museum.

SHIBUYA
渋谷

‣ **Shibuya is near Harajuku, Omotesando-dori, Aoyama, Yoyogi, Tomigaya, Daikanyama, Ebisu and Meiji-Jingu shrine.**

With its giant, luminous TV screens showing eye-popping ads, *Blade Runner*-esque lightscapes and impossible crowds, Shibuya cemented its pop-culture status long before the world came to snap pictures of it. This is an up-late precinct with a serious shopping addiction, a bubbling laboratory where worldwide trends, youth fashion and lifestyles are born. You'll find it all here – from seedy love hotels and game parlours to some of the world's best music venues, blockbuster art and, oh, did we mention shopping? Shibuya Scramble Square, Hikarie ShinQs and the newly revamped Parco are towering monuments to consumerism, while stalwarts Muji, Loft, Hands and Tower Records add a touch of pre-21st century character. The east side of Shibuya is the opposite of the frenzied west. Languid Cat Street is a great place for a lazy stroll on your way to Harajuku and in Jinan, a thriving network of backstreets hide some of Shibuya's best eating and independent retail.

SHIMOKITAZAWA
下北沢

‣ Shimokitazawa is near Shibuya, Setagaya, Meguro and Yoyogi.

Attempts by chain stores and high-rise developers to muscle in on Shimokita's flea-market charm have largely failed, and today this breezy enclave is on the rise again as one of Tokyo's most alluring non-conformist areas. Endearingly helter-skelter streets and alleyways hold wafer thin low-rise buildings with offbeat bars, unique record stores, miniscule craft galleries and cafes that do modern spins on Japanese staples. You'll find young Tokyo-ites rubbing shoulders with indie tourists rifling through racks at well-stocked thrift stores, relaxing in alfresco havens outside cafes or seating themselves at bars that look like they have grown organically overnight in shoebox-sized rooms. Weekend vintage shopping and people-watching in Shimokita has pretty much always been a Tokyo rite of passage, and its ongoing reputation as one of Tokyo's eccentric and energetic pockets is well deserved, so add it to your itinerary.

SHINJUKU
新宿

‣ Shinjuku is near Sendagaya, Harajuku, Yoyogi, Koenji and Shibuya.

Shinjuku is a chaotic city of stark contrasts. The station has 200 exits, and around 3.5 million people go through it every day so that should give you an idea of what you are in for. Sure, Shinjuku is a bit rough around the edges, but its manic nature makes it one of Tokyo's most popular destinations. Every brand, label and chain store have an outlet here, creating a seemingly endless crowd of shoppers. It's not all madness, though. Some truly beautiful relics of old Tokyo butt up against the colossal superstructures. Take some time out and stroll through peaceful Shinjuku Gyoen National Garden or head up the Metropolitan Government Building for a (free) view that stretches out to Mount Fuji. Float through the refined elegance of Isetan department store and make sure to spend some time in the memorable food hall. At night, immerse yourself in a remnant of postwar Tokyo, drinking at the quirky bars of the labyrinthinian Golden Gai and Omoide Yokocho.

SHIROKANEDAI
白金台

North-east of Meguro you'll find stylish and leafy Shirokanedai, perfect for a Sunday afternoon stroll or a green escape from the concrete jungle. Happo-en garden and the nearby Tokyo Metropolitan Teien Art Museum are some of Tokyo's best-kept secrets, destinations of great beauty and cultural interest that feel removed from the city's relentless energy. In fact, there are a plethora of fine museums, mostly exhibiting historical art and craft. Marvel at the Meiji Gakuin Shirokane university campus, which features some truly oddball mock Tudor-style buildings, completely out of place with the surroundings. Elsewhere, luxury fashion and designer homewares can be found in a host of upscale boutiques inhabiting some of Tokyo's quietest tree-lined streets.

‣ Shirokanedai is near Meguro and Ebisu.

TOKYO STATION SURROUNDS
東京駅周辺

Tokyo Station is not only a gateway for the shinkansen (bullet trains) that shoot off to every corner of Japan, the airport express and an alarming list of train lines (more than 4000 trains service the station daily), but also a frenetic, sprawling underground labyrinth. Exploring it will uncover myriad shops and restaurants, including the famed character street and Ramen Alley. You can lose hours here before you realise that you haven't even emerged into the outside world. When you do, you'll find one of Tokyo's most-enduring icons, the Imperial Palace, where the royal family reside to this day, and its delightful surrounding gardens. The gardens are worth exploring – and a welcome breath of fresh air – and there is a rich and royal history to uncover. Tokyo Station's west exit features a reimagining of the original 1914 frontage and includes some of the original structure and materials. It's a quick walk from here to Marunouchi, part business district and part cultural mecca, where some of Tokyo's most high-end shops can be found. Nearby Yurakucho, famous for its gado shita, or yokocho (small old-world eateries) under the train tracks, is a picturesque walk from Tokyo Station.

‣ Tokyo Station is near Marunouchi, Yurakucho, Ginza, Nihombashi, Kyobashi, Shimbashi and the Imperial Palace Gardens.

TOMIGAYA
富ヶ谷

Tomigaya long ago declared independence and seceded from neighbours Shibuya and Yoyogi, preferring to carve its own creative path, absorbing the breezy, relaxed feel of nearby Yoyogi park while ignoring the siren call of Shibuya's mad crowds. In a network of narrow streets, you'll find coffee houses, indie stores and a plethora of bars busting in on the remaining old-world tofu and fresh fish outlets. Clothing shops here sell understated separates, natural linens, and designs showcasing minimal silhouettes; excellent independent bookstores sell vintage tomes and local zines. While you're exploring Tomigaya, take a side-step to Yoyogi-Uehara, an area that grips tightly onto a late 20th-century atmosphere while slowly making way for the influx of the new.

‣ Tomigaya is near Yoyogi, Yoyogi-Uehara, Shibuya, Yoyogi park and the Mingeikan (The Japan Folk Crafts Museum).

UENO & YANESEN
上野&谷根千

Ueno and Yanesen's (Yanaka, Nezu and Sendagi) large parks, historic lanes and sleepy backstreets are steeped in the atmosphere of the Old Edo period (1603–1867). The shitemachi or 'low town' area was a merchant district with a clash of worker poverty and enthusiastic invention. In Ueno, Ameya Yokocho's winding market street harks back to the black-market era of post-World War II, and you'll find many stalls and hole-in-the-wall eateries. Nearby, peaceful Ueno park features some of Tokyo's finest museums and galleries in memorable architectural buildings. It's also home to one of Tokyo's best cherry blossom–viewing spots, best seen from cute swan boats that float under the pink canopies on lotus filled Shinobazu-no-ike pond. Moving further north, the surrounding streets and lanes are dotted with traditional paper makers, small restaurants and long-standing Mom and Pop stores. Don't miss Yanaka Cemetery or Yanaka Ginza, an old-school shopping street. The Nezu shrine is one of Tokyo's hidden gems, a less-visited shrine with a small vermilion torii gate tunnel. Note that the Skyliner train goes from Ueno to Narita Airport, so if you need to while away hours before travelling, put your bag in a locker and explore the area.

‣ Ueno and Yanasen are near Nippori, Asakusa and Akihabara.

YOYOGI
代々木

‣ Yoyogi is near Tomigaya, Shibuya, Harajuku, Shinjuku, Omotesando-dori and the Meiji-Jingu shrine.

The sprawling and beautiful Yoyogi park is a major cherry blossom and picnic destination that served as the site for the Tokyo Olympics in 1964. Yoyogi National Stadium, designed by Kenzo Tange for the games, is a mid-century architectural masterpiece and a must-visit for culture and sporting buffs. The area is famous for the outrageous dress-ups of the Harajuku kids and the preening struts of old rock 'n' rollers on Sunday afternoons and although this has subsided somewhat, some of the fun can still be experienced as you head towards Harajuku station. Yoyogi seems to have sprouted organically around the park and has quickly become a neighbourhood that feels a lot like Tokyo's answer to Brooklyn. It's all about books, coffee and design and afternoon go-slows where people gather in cafes and chat about their latest zine or website project. Hire a bicycle and make a day of it or grab a bento and go for a picnic in the park!

SPECIALIST TOWNS

Embedded within Tokyo's sprawling expanse, you'll find little themed 'towns' that have developed their own specialties over time and have been named accordingly. Here you can find everything from the tranquil Cat Town full of lazy street cats to Book Town for bibliophiles and Electric Town for gadget geeks. Take the opportunity to spend a day exploring an area that seems to have been made just for you!

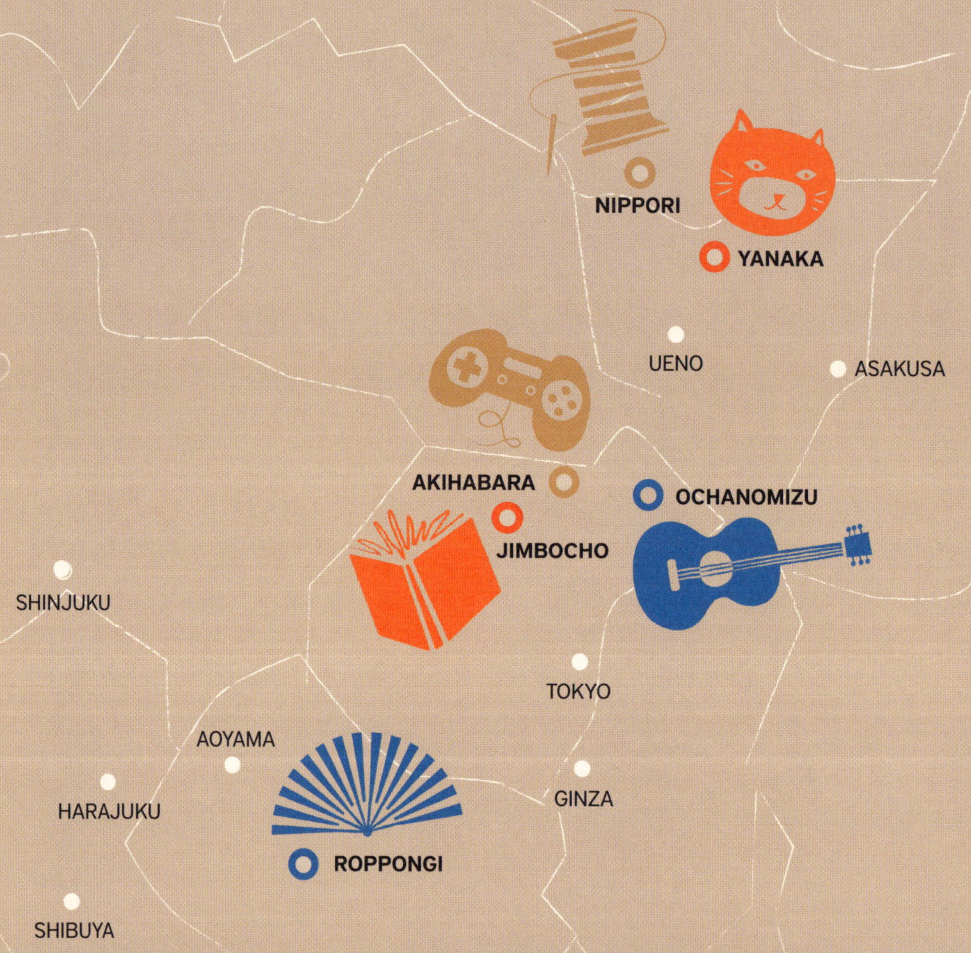

CAT TOWN
猫の街

Yanaka

Yanaka's gentle neighbourhood vibes have made it the purr-fect home to clowders of street cats. Prowling around alleys and sunning themselves in front of cafes, the local felines claim this precinct lost in time as their own and will accompany you on your wander like protective gods (albeit furry, hungry ones). Start at **Ueno park**, maybe taking in an exhibition at a gallery or museum, before heading north. You'll pass **Kayaba**, a classic coffee house, and **Scai The Bathhouse**, no longer a sento, now a gallery showing the latest contemporary art. Sprawling **Tokugawa Yanaka Cemetery** is here as well, an excellent spot for cherry blossoms. **Yanaka Ginza** is breezy and historic with old-world shopping and small shrines that pepper the narrow streets. You'll see why the cats have adopted the area; trinket shops and souvenir stands are dominated by feline motifs, so stock up on cat merchandise. Heading south from Yanaka Ginza, stop to refuel at **CIBI Tokyo Store** before heading to **Isetatsu**, a long-standing paper store selling sheets of chiyogami (screen-printed paper) made in the traditional Edo style. Then continue south towards **Nezu shrine** for an afternoon's contemplation amongst the red torii gates and colourful seasonal plantings.

FABRIC TOWN
生地の街

Nippori

Calling all material girls (and boys) and sews-ciopaths, follow the thread to Nippori, headquarters of the craft mafia. Self-styled as Fabric Town, Nippori is a part of Tokyo that has been dedicated to cloth and sewing materials since the early Taisho period (1912–26) and it retains much of the charm of that era. Michelle will set aside a whole day, wandering the streets in search of thick linens, indigo dyed fabric and hemp and fawning over elegant rinzu silks (used in making kimono). Fabrics, lace, ribbons, buttons and bows can also be found in over 90 stores that line the Nippori streets and, in particular, along **Nippori Main Street**, sprouting out of the south exit of Nippori station. Most stores open at 11am but can be closed on weekends, so always check websites for times. We recommend stalwart **Tomato** (taking up much of the real estate on the main street with multiple stores), **Humongous**, **On-Travelling**, **Nipporiomaru** (for beads) and for specifically Japanese patterned fabric, **Mihama** and **Tsukiyasu**. You can pick up a fabric town store map in English from Nippori station's information booth. Many fabric stores are shut on a Sunday.

ELECTRIC TOWN
電気街

Akihabara

Looking for a domestic robot servant or an invisible drone – you probably won't be able to find them here ... yet. Akiba, as it is affectionately known, is the Tokyo mecca for tech nerds, gamers, anime fans and figurine collectors. Of course, it's now cool to collect and you won't be beaten up by bullies in Akihabara unless you are in the way of a collector of a rare Astro Boy figurine (mint in box) or first edition of manga Shonen Jump. One thing that really draws the crowds here is Electric Town, a criss-cross rabbit warren of tiny stores sitting amongst the tech giants selling the very latest, up-to-the-minute and often mind-boggling gadgetry. Plan to spend the better part of your day (and your budget) here at mega versions of chain stores like **Yodobashi Camera**, **Sofmap**, **Bic Camera** and **Laox** but make sure to wind in and out of the smaller stores, where you'll find a wide range of electronic specialties stacked to the ceiling on shelves and crammed into cabinets. Always remember that they will mostly be using Japanese plugs and wattage, so budget to get a conversion or to buy a transformer.

BOOK TOWN
本の街

Jimbocho

This book is our Tokyo story, but Jimbocho is the town where Tokyo's stories live. Named after a local samurai, Nagaharu Jimbo, and with a history dating back to the 17th century that includes being almost completely wiped out in the great fire of 1913, Jimbocho's own story rivals the stories in many of the books that literally spill out of the shelves of the 120 bookstores that line its streets. If you want to feel the crisp leaves of a weighty hardback between your fingers and smell the dusty pages of tomes gone by, Jimbocho will certainly have what you need. You'll leaf through mostly vintage books, some startlingly old, as well as parchments, scrolls and posters, but the pop-culture lover will be delighted by the '80s music magazines and '70s postcards. Both Japanese and Western texts, including English language, are available, crammed onto moody shelves in dark curiosity shops and piled up on the floor, teetering on the brink of collapse. Try book superstore **Sanseido** and antiquarian favourite **Isseido**. **Ohya Shobo**'s rare book collection and **Bohemian's Guild**'s focus on art and design books are favourites of ours. Of course, in a town of books, it naturally follows that there are plenty of students in Jimbocho, and therefore a plethora of cheap but cheerful curry and ramen joints, too!

MUSIC TOWN
音楽の街

Ochanomizu

If music be the food of love, you'll leave Ochanomizu needing some Buscopan and a diet plan. It's everywhere, if not playing in the live houses or rehearsal spaces, then certainly forming in the minds of the many musicians who wander the area, wide-eyed, waiting to unearth that much-sought-after vintage guitar and start shredding. Over 50 music shops dot the streets here, like crochets and quavers. Seek out classic guitars: Fender, Gretsch and Rickenbacker on Meidai Guitar St, which has more guitars than Johnny Marr's lounge room. They're in stores and spilling out onto the streets forming a serious overall cache which makes the whole town look like a guitar museum. **Shimokura Second Hand Guitar Shop**, **Ishibashi Music**, **BigBoss** and **Kurosawa** are all favourite pitstops of Steve's. Japanese-only brands like Fujigen, Tokai and Caparison give a masterclass in handmade instruments that come in unique shapes and wood varieties. With a vast range of accessories on offer including effects pedals, amps and strings, Ochanomizu will strike a chord with any music obsessive, but make sure you get the flying V out of there before you spend two months' wage.

ART TOWN
アートの街

Roppongi

In a city of over 14 million people, there has to be a place to go and get loose and Roppongi is it. Crowds throng the streets, questionable girl bars, clubs and all-night eateries inhabit the upper floors of sketchy skyscrapers, and freeways and bypasses teeter on concrete pillars, roads stretching into oblivion. When Sunday morning comes, the place could certainly do with a good bath. But in recent years Roppongi has become decidedly schizophrenic. Concept mini city **Tokyo Midtown** and the sprawling, labyrinthine **Azabudai Hills** have given Roppongi a luxe edge that belies its grimy reputation and this is further enhanced by the Roppongi Art Triangle. **Mori Art Museum**, **National Art Center** and **Suntory Museum of Art** are all unmissable destinations for the connoisseur, and the addition of the sharply conceived **21_21 Design Sight**, willed into existence by fashion designer par excellence Issey Miyake (the building being designed by superstar architect Tadao Ando), has made this walkable 'triangle' one of the world's premiere art destinations. Annual events including Roppongi Art Night, and installations and sculptures are dotted about the streets to remind you that this precinct now has a taste for the higher visual arts.

SPECIALIST STREETS

Just as many of Tokyo's 'towns' have their own special themes, some streets in the city also have their own personality. For example, head to the kitchenwear hub of Kappabashi-dori, the luxe stores of Omotesando-dori or the indie designer shopping and foodie laneways of Kichijoji. A jaunt down one of these famous strips is an unmissable part of your Tokyo encounter.

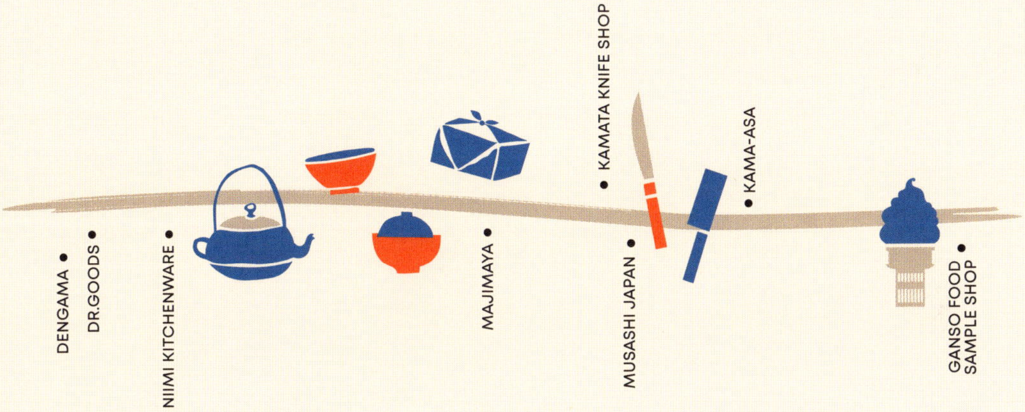

KAPPABASHI-DORI
合羽橋通り

Asakusa

Tokyo has an astonishing 80,000-plus restaurants, and Kappabashi-dori is where the owners and chefs come to shop. This thoroughfare will literally 'cater' to your every need. Look up to see the giant chef's head with the perfectly coiffured moustache and the towering teacups of the **Niimi** store and you'll know you're entering the biggest cookware shopping street in the world. Prices are low and the variety is large. Each store presents a mind-boggling array of ceramics, crockery, utensils, chopsticks, chef uniforms, tableware and just about anything else you can think of that relates to the art, or business, of cookery. Kettles and coffee pots line the shelves and copper and enamel pots, artisan bamboo steamers and taiyaki (fish-shaped pastry) makers, are some of our favourite buys. You'll find chopstick holders, cookie cutters, furoshiki (cloth wrapping) and bento boxes perfect to take home or give as gifts. For kitchen knives, **Majimaya**, **DR.GOODS**, **Musashi Japan**, **Kama-Asa** and **Kamata Knife Shop** are unmissable stores. **Dengama** is exceptional for ceramics. A must-buy in Kappabashi is the sampuru (from the English word 'sample'), plastic display food that adorns the windows of many Japanese restaurants. They range from the functional to the fabulous, the comical to the disturbing. Like little pop-art sculptures, they make interesting gifts or souvenirs. You can buy large models, or tiny sampuru keyrings from **Ganso Food Sample Shop**.

SUN ROAD ARCADE
サンロード商店街

Kichijoji

A short walk from the north exit of Kichijoji station leads to Sun Road, a network of covered arcades that feature a concentration of local shops, thrift stores and small eateries and food stalls, many of which are open to the street, giving Sun Road Arcade the feel of a hawkers market. Meat shop **Satou Butchers** sell grilled mincemeat sets, a lunch that is hugely popular with locals and visitors, and the shop's ever-present queue snakes past premium tea and pickle shops. Well-priced clothes shops and shoe stores, kitchenalia stores and novelty shops share space with a plethora of yakitori, tonkatsu (breadcrumb pork) and ramen joints. Standout moments include ornate, eccentric **Coffee Hall Kugutsuso**, **Amane Taiyaki** down a small alley off the arcade (try the purple sweet potato filling) and rambling **Kikuya** for kitchenalia. Sun Road also features free wi-fi and a recent refurbishment has dragged it into the 21st century, possibly losing some of its outdated, shabby charm along the way.

NAKAMICHI-DORI
中道通り

Kichijoji

Nakamichi-dori in the jaunty neighbourhood of Kichijoji is the perfect street for an afternoon stroll. It's both relaxing and inspiring popping in and out of shops that feature the work of creative handcrafters, small fashion designers and dedicated vintage curators. Spend a few hours in **Wickie** for crafty and vintage finds and if you find yourself with ESD (Extreme Stationery Disorder), don't miss **Paper Message** and **Giovanni**. If you're looking to send letters or parcels head to **Pack Mart**, an old-fashioned stationery shop with cramped aisles brimming with postage bags, tape and things that wrap, bind and bundle. The blue striped exterior of **Coeur de Coeur** will draw you into a shop that sells an adorable range of stationery and vintage homewares. Up a steep flight of stairs you'll find **Free Design**, a tiny space crammed with homewares and novelties. **Kichijoji Petit Mura** is fun, an enclave of small sweets shops all with fairytale theme designs. Stop to refuel at **Namaste Kathmandu** (a highly rated Indian/Nepalese eatery with many vegetarian options). Or take a sharp right into the street called Country Road, for a curry at the '70s Kichijoji classic **Mamezo**. Peruse the immaculate homewares at **Markus** or clothing at **Natural Laundry** while you are there. Choose your favourite brew at **Light Up Coffee**, **Capoon Matcha Café** or **Tototo & Soymilk** to have with one of our favourite Tokyo sweet treats from **Hara Donuts**. Nearby Showa-dori is also worth a look, of note are indie darlings **Niji Gallery** and **Book Mansion**.

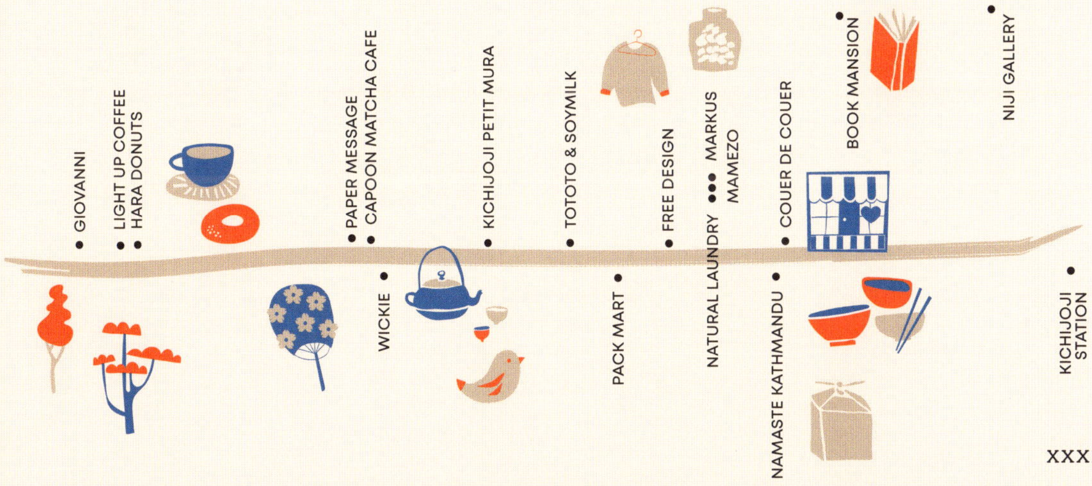

CAT STREET
キャットストリート

Harajuku

A slinky catwalk linking frenetic Shibuya and Harajuku, Cat Street has the latest fashion, food and shopping at your fingertips. With a lazy Sunday feel no matter what day you are there, a TV vox pop or fashion photo shoot always seems to be going on. There are no actual cats (the closest thing you'll find is the Puma store), but there's plenty of preening and grooming among the cool Tokyo-ites. Head into **The Roastery by Nozy Coffee** or **The Matcha** for a quick energy hit and a spot of human watching before assaulting **RAGTAG** and raiding its racks for upscale vintage. **G.B. Gafas** makes sophisticated spectacles. Ironically, given that cats are so lazy, there are plenty of sporting and outdoor goods shops along the strip. Your whiskers will be twitching by now as you smell the takoyaki (octopus dumplings) at **WaraTako** or why not slink into the side streets for a gyoza fix at **Gyoza-ro** and to hunt out the vast mod cavern of **Fred Perry**, where you'll find sharp Japanese-only versions of the iconic English label. Don't miss visiting **Shu Uemura**'s flagship store, designed to resemble a giant black make-up box. At the end of your Cat Street parade, you'll merge onto the mad rush of Omotesando-dori, and just to your right you'll find multi-level toy store **Kiddy Land** and the **GYRE** building.

OMOTESANDO-DORI
表参道通り

Harajuku

It's unlikely that you'll be able to avoid braving the crowds of Omotesando-dori at some point during any visit to Tokyo – it's just that iconic. Stretching from Harajuku all the way down to Aoyama, the wide boulevard is Tokyo's stab at the Champs-Élysées. The street says everything you need to know about upscale, over-the-top contemporary Tokyo. Impressive architecture is everywhere – from youth fashion mecca **La Foret** to the mirrored shards of **Tokyu Plaza Omokado**, the verdant forest rooftop of **Tokyu Plaza Harakado**, the out-of-place **Tokyo Union Church** and the modern brutalism of Tadao Ando's concrete bunker **Omotesando Hills**. Both high-end and low-end shopping experiences collide on the main drag, including the ever-popular **Kiddy Land** and destination department store **GYRE**. The streets will likely be thronging with people, especially on a weekend or a holiday, when the sheer scope of the crowd is jaw-dropping, particularly when viewed from the top end of Harajuku. Much further down you leave the madness behind for the relative calm of Aoyama. Take a slight detour to **Higashiya Man** for a takeout manju (sweet red bean paste filled bun). The narrower, more strollable streets feature boutique fashion stores including the famous **Prada** green glass tower and the inventive, quirky **COMME des GARÇONS**, which will always have a sculptural piece of art in its gallery-like front windows. **Issey Miyake** makes his mark on the street with a plethora of different stores with various themes. Finally, just when you feel like capitalism has ensnared you in its multifarious tentacles, the tranquil gardens of the **Nezu Museum** bring you a much-needed escape.

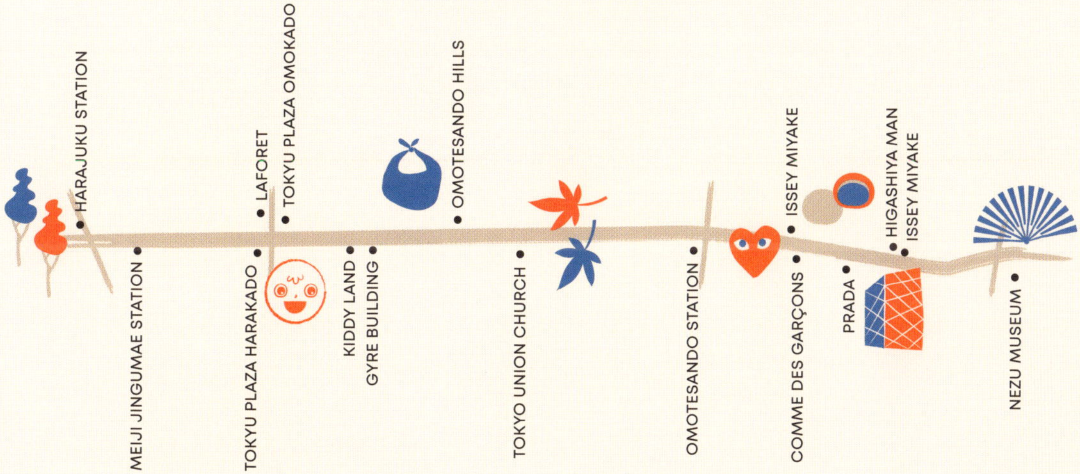

Tokyo is a frenetic, pulsating city where pedestrians crowd the sidewalks and cars and trains provide an endless symphony/cacophony of city noise. The pace is relentless and cramming your to-do list into a timeframe can be an exhausting experience. It is a city of contrasts however, and counteracting the daily chaos are many spiritual and mindful practices to soothe the body and quiet the mind.

We like to relax by doing classes in, for instance, the ancient art of kintsugi (visible repair), or by having a contemplative cup of tea in one of the city's historic teahouses or tea salons, some of which are in quiet backstreets so it feels as though you are stepping back in time. You can also experience a traditional tea ceremony.

If you want to dive deeper into really relaxing in Tokyo however, one of our very favourite things is to have a relaxing soak in one of the many sento bathhouses. They're usually an inside affair — you won't find sweeping views or ancient baths hewn from rock or built from local pine as you would further out in the Japanese countryside. However, there are excellent baths in the middle of the city, sometimes for less than the price of a coffee, and they can't be beaten when you need to relax those overworked sightseeing muscles. Also, in a city with an astounding range of food options, why not indulge in a spot of mindful eating, like a delicious vegan ramen or tofu feast?

All of these places will help you experience a mega city with a difference where centuries of expertise in purity, harmony and relaxation serve to invigorate the traveller.

TOKYO

東京物語

MINDFUL

MAENOHARA SAYANO YUDOKORO

前野原温泉
さやの湯処

Itabashi

3-41-1 Maenocho, Itabashi-ku

Mon–Sun 9am–12am

‣ Shimura-Sakaue station, exit A2

sayanoyudokoro.co.jp

An updated Showa period (1926–89) building with a beautiful Zen garden sets the scene for this stylish neighbourhood onsen featuring hot springs, sauna, massage and food experiences. The superb quality of the water gives you all the benefits of a mineral-rich country spring without you having to leave the city. According to Maenohara, it is the only Tokyo onsen that links directly to the source, with water pumped up from 1500m below. Jet baths and the 'water-seats' – stone chairs with cascades of warm flowing water – are wonderfully relaxing. Outside a pagoda covers a large milky white rotenburo (outside onsen). There are also smaller 'pot' baths, good for solo bathing, where water is the colour of olive green or yellow minerals. At night the garden looks almost fairy-like and lanterns with soft yellow light hug the pathways. For an extra fee, try the bedrock sauna or indulge in a Japanese 'temomi,' a Korean body scrub or aromatherapy massage. Private relaxing tatami rooms are available for an hourly fee, or head to the communal tatami area for a cosy lie down. After your first, second or third bath, stroll through the winding wooden corridors to the restaurant where a beautiful tatami mat room looks over the Zen garden. Make sure you try their specialty, Juwari soba, consisting of 100 per cent buckwheat noodles, while you gaze over perfectly arranged rocks and greenery.

CULTURE NOTE

Those with small tattoos can buy cover stickers — although if two stickers aren't enough to cover your ink, then you won't be allowed in.

SENTO IN TOKYO
東京の銭湯

Mostly opening around midday and remaining open long into the night, Tokyo's inner-city sento come in a wide range of sizes and experiences. Most bathhouses will be sento: built baths with the minerals added manually and brightly coloured murals on the walls, usually depicting Mount Fuji or scenes of city life. However, you'll find the occasional onsen which are more rustic (they often also cost more), with natural thermal mineral water pumped up from springs far below the ground.

Fully renovated in 2014, **Komeisen** (Nakameguro station, west exit) is a chic and contemporary sento that retains a classic feel. Perfectly placed in the chill backstreets of Nakameguro, this upstart is the ideal urban local hangout for a spot of relaxation. Jiyugaoka's **Midori-yu** (Jiyugaoka station, south exit), established in 1957, has walls that feature mountain motifs, including the ubiquitous Mount Fuji. There is a sauna and a cold plunge bath along with small hot water baths that change with the seasons. If you are looking for a local sento with a gorgeous vintage old-world frontage, charming aesthetic elements and clean, quality baths, head to **Inari-yu** (Ikebukuro station, exit 35). The spotless bathhouse with a tiled Mount Fuji mosaic and wooden bath bowls is a treat — so much so that they shot scenes for the bathhouse-themed comedy film *Thermae Romae* (2012) here. Basking under the watchful eye of the Skytree, you'll find **Daikoku-yu** (Kinshicho station, exit 4). This small, character-filled onsen pumps water from a well that was discovered over 60 years ago. It features jet baths, seated baths and herb baths as well as a 90cm deep bath warmed to 35ºC (95ºF), which is perfect for muscle rehabilitation. Murals inside depict Kyoto's Kinkaku-ji golden pavilion and a pastoral scene from Nikko. Head out onto the wooden deck where you can relax with a (partial) view of the Skytree, one of the few from a public bath. At **Tsubame-yu** (Okachimachi station, south exit), you can admire the blue canopied entrance and inside you'll find a small rock garden and a large painting of Mount Fuji presiding over a handful of relaxing baths. It opens at 6am for early risers looking for a relaxing start to the day and it features volcanic rock from Mount Fuji. Recently refurbished **Mikoku-yu** (Ryogoku station, exit A2), founded in 1947, also features a partial Skytree view and is proud of its eco stance, utilising rainwater where possible. You should also seek out the impressive Showa period (1926—89) frontage of **Kotobuki-yu** (Inaricho station, exit 3), whose small but alluring baths often feature a rotation of medicinal herbs. **Tsuruno-yu** (Kuramae station, exit A3) has a powder-blue frontage and impressive gabled entrance that leads you into a sento known for medicinal baths and a silky-white bath with nano-bubbles. **Akebono-yu** (Asakusa station, exit 6) features some excellent jet baths, but it's the intricate roof and ornate frontage and foyer decorations that make this a real standout. Don't stop here however: many of Tokyo's neighbourhoods are brimming with sento and onsen just waiting for you to fully immerse yourself in the culture of bathing. One of our very favourites is the ultra cute retro **Misuji-yu** in Kuramae (Kuramae Station, exit 3).

Always check ahead but, in our experience, most of the local sentos have no problem with tattoos (we have seen some astounding body art in some of these sento).

CULTURE NOTE

Don't miss Tokyo's impressive range of contemporary sento. Head to **Kogane-yu** (Kinshicho station, exit 3), **Sway Sauna** (Gaienmae station, exit 3), and nearby **Paradise** (Gaienmae station, exit 3).

KOSOAN
古桑庵

Jiyugaoka

1-24-23 Jiyugaoka, Meguro-ku

Mon–Tues & Thurs–Fri 12–6.30pm, Sat–Sun 11am–6.30pm

‣ Jiyugaoka station, main exit

kosoan.co.jp

Just north of Jiyugaoka station, past the modern shops and cafes, you'll find yourself suddenly stepping back in time as the pace slows and the shops and buildings give way to greenery and quiet backstreets. Kosoan will appear suddenly at the side of the road, a mystical villa with a small landscape garden with classic motifs of moss, pine, azaleas, maples, bamboo and water features. The building, repurposed from a residence over 100 years old, is built from mulberry wood and features historical elements like tatami mats, alcoves for shrines and sliding shoji (screen doors of glass and wood). The teahouse has a simple menu, which includes matcha and sweets, and anmitsu, a Meiji period (1868–1912) dessert of agar jelly, fruit, mochi and red bean paste, enjoyed by couples on dates and locals enjoying a slow afternoon. A tranquil haven, Kosoan is a lovely spot to stop for tea, soak in the traditional surroundings and feel, just for a moment, like you aren't in one of the world's biggest and busiest cities.

HAPPO-EN
八芳園

Shirokanedai

1-1-1 Shirokanedai, Minato-ku

Fri–Tues 11am–6pm

‣ Shirokanedai station, exit 2

happo-en.com

Happo-en was founded over 80 years ago as a restaurant in residence in an Edo period (1603–1867) garden that was designed to reflect the changing of each season in stunning floral and foliage displays. The name means 'Garden of eight views,' appropriate as the wonders in this garden are stunning from many angles. Water features, rockeries and a beautiful display of bonsai, some up to 500 years old, are just some of the delights in this peaceful oasis tucked away amid the broad streets and frenetic traffic of Meguro. For a relaxing experience, book the tea ceremony in the front room of Meiji period (1868–1912) teahouse **Mu-an**, where you can order a light meal of delicious green tea and wagashi (Japanese sweets) and enjoy it with a view of the lake teeming with some truly impressive koi. However, if you want to go for the full ceremony experience, take the Edo romance garden walk, a tour of the garden complete with an elaborate tea ceremony and dinner in the restaurant. With all this beauty, it's no wonder that Happo-en is the chosen site for many weddings (apparently it hosts over 1000 per year).

DESIGN NOTE

Nearby **Zuisho-ji temple**, over 355 years old, has an impressive addition to the priest quarters designed by Kengo Kuma.

IPPODO
一保堂

Marunouchi

Shin-Marunouchi Building B1F, 1-5-1 Marunouchi, Chiyoda-ku

Mon–Sat 11am–8pm, Sun 11am–7pm

‣ Tokyo Station, Marunouchi north exit

global.ippodo-tea.co.jp

Connected to the huge hub of Tokyo Station by underground passages, the basement of the Shin-Marunouchi Building is a blur of office workers getting from A to Z. Thankfully they can now stop for tea in between. The most famous tea brand in Kyoto, Ippodo, has been perfecting the art of tea since 1717. Their new Tokyo store is a stunning minimal space accented by warm woods and concrete with an eye-catching frontage of scalloped noren (traditional curtains) dyed with tea leaves, that mimic the flow of the wind. The interior features lighting by Kojima Shoten that resembles large floating clouds, plus curved walls, display pods and tea-making stations. The main counter is an impressive single slab of chestnut. Join the counter queue and order a matcha to go. It's uncommon to get tea of this quality to take away so take note while the staff slowly scoop and whisk hot water into the matcha bowl until a bright emerald tea sits before you. Tea varieties are extensive and served in adorable graphic print cups. Try Gyokuro, a type of Japanese green tea grown in shade rather than sun. Steve loves the smokey Iribancha, but everyone else lines up for a choice of thick or regular matcha, and the popular hojicha latte. Don't leave without a bamboo scoop (chashaku), tea whisk (chasen), bowl (chawan) or packaged tea, all perfect take-home gifts.

DESIGN NOTE

Renowned design firm ima used natural materials like paper, fabric and wood to evoke the feeling of a forest oasis. Branding studio CICATA, Inc. have just updated Ippodo's packaging range.

HIGASHIYA
ヒガシヤ

Ginza

Pola Building 2F,
1-7-7 Ginza, Chuo-ku

Mon–Sun 11am–3pm & 5–9pm

‣ Ginza station, exit A13

higashiya.com

It's easy to walk past Ginza's Pola Building without knowing the treasure that lies within, but the luxurious Higashiya on the 2nd floor is a tea salon that anyone interested in exploring Tokyo tea culture cannot miss. The interior is classic Japanese with a minimal architectural makeover. Choose a bench seat or sit at a table and watch the expert staff pour hot water from giant copper kettles into bowls and then whisk in rich green matcha. Delectable lunch sets are served in equally delectable ceramics, or you can opt for afternoon tea and delicate wagashi (Japanese sweets). We are partial to both experiences. There are over 30 varieties of tea to choose from, all perfect when accompanied by delicate mochi (sweet rice cakes), which are arranged in boxes like tiny gems. If you are short on time, the small shop at the entrance sells Higashiya's specialist tea, sweets and elegant homewares. The sweets are an optical delight and make perfect gifts for friends and family.

SAKURAI JAPANESE TEA EXPERIENCE
櫻井培茶研究所

Aoyama

Spiral Building 5F,
5-6-23 Minami Aoyama,
Minato-ku

Mon–Sun 11am–8pm

‣ Omotesando station, exit B1

sakurai-tea.jp

After 14 years perfecting his craft, tea master Shinya Sakurai opened the teahouse Sakurai where he presents a contemporary version of the traditional tea ceremony. Housed on the refurbished 5th floor of the Spiral Building in the chic Aoyama/Omotesando area, it's an exceptional date venue or place to take your architecture or design-obsessed friends. Every part of the visually stunning tearoom is carefully crafted and considered, including the exquisite signage. The minimalist space is accented by brass and polished concrete. The glass sink is a notable feature, with a shimmering waterfall disappearing into its shallow bowl. You will be shown to a counter seat overlooking a square bench where the tea master will work his magic for all to see, whisking, agitating and pouring – tea making that commands silence. Hojicha (tea) is roasted in store and seasonal varieties are brewed using elaborate kettles and teapots and poured into elegant ceramics. Varieties are drawn from the best tea regions in Japan and blended to perfection. Enjoy your tea with some of Tokyo's most artfully made seasonal wagashi (Japanese sweets) while you gaze out over the Aoyama skyline, especially romantic as the sun sets and Sakurai begin to mix their excellent tea-infused cocktails.

FOODIE NOTE

Higashiya Man in Aoyama is a hole-in-the-wall shop selling freshly made manju (steamed buns).

TEA NOTE

Yamamotoyama Fuji Sabo is an elegant contemporary teahouse in Nihonbashi.

TOKOAN AT IMPERIAL HOTEL
帝国ホテル 東光庵

Hibiya

Imperial Hotel 4F,
1-1-1 Uchisaiwaicho,
Chiyoda-ku

Mon–Sat 10am–4pm

‣ Hibiya station, exit A13

imperialhotel.co.jp

The grand, stately and decidedly luxe Imperial is one of Tokyo's most-revered hotels. Surprisingly, it features a traditional-style teahouse on the 4th floor. The Tokoan tea ceremony space is no mere room, but a perfectly realised re-creation of a traditional Sukiya-style teahouse with a classic three-chambered structure. Architectural excellence imbues it with a sense of the contemporary, yet heading inside the tearoom from the Western-style Imperial Hotel hallway is a bit of a shock, as it seems to be a room out of time and place – and that is the intention. It is designed to take you out of the everyday and to a more refined, sophisticated world, like that of a classical teahouse in the deep countryside. Walk along the perfectly placed stones, letting the low lighting and subtle atmosphere set the mood. Sit and meditate upon the space, with its various chambers leading to anterooms, the musty-sweet smell of tatami rising up and mingling with the heady aroma of tea. Your host, demonstrating the pinnacle of chado omotenashi (the deep and open-hearted care of the guest) will float delicately around the space, each subtle flick of the wrist and movement of the hands divulging another part of the wonderful chado tea ceremony.

YAKUMO SARYO
八雲茶寮

Yakumo

3-4-7 Yakumo, Meguro-ku

Mon–Sun 9am–4pm

‣ Toritsu-daigaku station, south exit

yakumosaryo.jp

Walking the quiet backstreets of Yakumo, just north of Jiyugaoka, unearths an exquisite treasure: a destination restaurant with a transportive tea experience. White noren (traditional curtains) beckon you into a tranquil enclave, imagined by Shinichiro Ogata of revered design studio Simplicity. Conceptually this is Ogata's salon of cultural exchange, where detail and craftsmanship are blended with purity and innovation. Experiences range from a small gallery, **Salon**, to **Baishinka**, their store selling beautifully boxed wagashi (Japanese sweets). You can have a multi-course Japanese breakfast or lunch or participate in a tea course at **Sabo** teahouse. In the low afternoon light, the dark haven of Sabo is a delightfully moody experience. The materiality of the room features warm wood, brushed concrete and mixed metals, as beautifully blended as the tea served within. One large table becomes the setting for a tea experience that includes cultivated ceramics, perfectly selected and blended tea and a delicate seasonal sweet. Booking for breakfast and lunch are a must (dinner is by invitation only).

HISTORY NOTE

Frank Lloyd Wright designed the second incarnation of Tokyo's Imperial Hotel. Designed in the Maya Revival Style, it opened in June 1923 and famously survived the Great Kanto earthquake in September 1923. It was partly destroyed in World War II and sadly demolished in 1967.

KUNGYOKUDO
薫玉堂

Marunouchi

KITTE Marunouchi
4F, 2-7-2 Marunouchi,
Chiyoda-ku

Sun–Fri 11am–8pm

‣ Tokyo Station,
Marunouchi exit

kungyokudo.co.jp

One of the ways we include mindfulness in our everyday life is through the meditative experience of lighting incense in our home. The wafting scent plays a powerful experiential role in taking us back to Japan to forest walks or spiritual temple visits. Kungyokudo is Japan's oldest incense brand with over 430 years of history creating incense for temples – dating back to 1594 in Kyoto as apothecary supplier to Nishi Hongan-ji temple. Remarkably, its flagship store in Tokyo is in the Kengo Kuma architecturally refurbished and very contemporary KITTE building (*see* p. 34). The carefully considered, understated modern apothecary store design, exquisite packaging and product selection is the perfect juxtaposition of the ancient world meeting the modern city. With centuries-old recipes, their scented products range from oils and soaps to grooming items and their signature incense. We encourage you when entering the store to shut your eyes and imagine the scent of Japan hundreds of years ago. Kungyokudo have literally bottled and stylishly packaged the temple fragrances through the ages, so that you can be instantly transported to those gentler times.

HISTORY NOTE

Kungyokudo's 22nd-generation family owners Kazuo Ouno and his wife Chihaya Ouno use the original techniques to reaffirm the quality and care of their signature scents. Their renowned skills as a historical incense store and supplier ensure that many temples across Japan use their superior product.

KYU ASAKURA HOUSE
旧朝倉家住宅

Daikanyama

29-20 Sarugakucho, Shibuya-ku

Tues–Sun 10am–4.30pm

‣ Daikanyama station, central exit

city.shibuya.tokyo.jp

Kyu Asakura House has quietly stood in breezy, gentrified Daikanyama for over a century, its elegant story unfolding long before the chic fashion boutiques and restaurants arrived. One train stop away from busy Shibuya, you'll be transported into a rare pocket of quiet that instantly evokes the feeling of old Tokyo. Finished in 1919 for the prominent Asakura family, the house was designed in the Meiji period style (1868–1912). This architectural gem is a rare example of wood and tatami craftsmanship, largely lost after the Great Kanto earthquake in September 1923 and subsequent World War II bombings. Its moss-covered wooden entrance and pathway guide visitors to the main entrance, where, upon stepping inside, you're invited to remove your shoes and wander the creaking wooden corridors. Through open shoji screens, you'll catch glimpses of the meticulously designed Japanese garden, where each tree, rock and lantern is placed to create the perfect view – nature as art. Our favourite season to visit is winter, when the low afternoon light fills the interior with a warm, golden glow. Kyu Asakura house is a Japanese Important Cultural Property. Look out for the masterful 1st floor cedar rooms, designed in the Sukiya-Zashiki style.

KUGE CRAFTS
手仕事屋久家

Shin-Koenji

1-34-10 Narita-higashi, Suginami-ku

Hours vary

‣ Shin-Koenji station, exit 1

teshigotoya-kuge.com

To mend a cherished object with gold joinery is a time-honoured Japanese craft that requires patience, skill and care. The art of kintsugi (visible repair) honours the object by giving it a new life, rather than discarding it. More than just repairing something that is broken, kintsugi takes on the mantle of a multi-layered metaphor, a method of 'visible mending' that open-heartedly says that an object's cracks and flaws should be highlighted, and thus the broken thing proudly shows its scars. Yoshiichiro sensei and Yoshiko sensei have taught ceramics and kintsugi for over 40 years and will instruct you on how to mould putty into a break, painting it with lacquer when it has hardened and sprinkling it with gold dust for beauty and delicacy. There are many levels of workshops, most involving commitment, but they also offer a 2.5hr small group express class for novice craft enthusiasts. Bring a treasured broken plate if you want and watch it take on a new, imperfectly perfect life before your eyes. Class times are listed online and should be booked in advance.

AREA NOTE

If you're intrigued by Japanese architecture, a visit to **T-Site** (*see* p. 169) across the street could be the perfect opportunity to pick up a book for further research, while also providing a contemporary architectural contrast.

DESIGN NOTE

You can also drop off a piece for the Kuge sensei to expertly repair for you.

TOFU CUISINE SORANO
豆腐料理 空野

Shibuya

4-17 Sakuragaokacho, Shibuya-ku

Mon–Sun 5–11pm

‣ Shibuya station, east exit

foodgate.net/shop/sorano

On a narrow street running alongside the Shonan-Shinjuku line train tracks from Shibuya, you'll come upon an out-of-place restaurant with a stylish entrance and long noren (traditional curtains) that invite you to float in and walk along a stone pathway. Inside, follow the pebble path past water features and wooden stairs to one of the semi-private tatami rooms. Tofu Cuisine Sorano have a contemporary take on a traditional interior and a contemporary approach to traditional food. Make sure you request the fresh tofu, which makes the journey from soy milk to tofu at your table. There's nothing quite like the freshest tofu 'grown' at your table with no embellishment but a drizzle of premium soy sauce. Dishes like the creamy avocado tofu, or crispy fried yuba (tofu skin) will likely convert the most die-hard tofu opponent. Most dishes are well priced, and drinks include a delicious soy cocktail, or Michelle's favourite: the sake cocktail with small apricot pieces. The tofu even extends to dessert; the tiramisu and the cheesecake are deliciously good. Whilst a wonderful restaurant for vegetarians and vegans, there are also meat dishes on the menu.

TOFU UKAI
とうふ屋うかい

Shiba-Koen

4-4-13 Shiba-Koen, Minato-ku

Mon–Sun 11am–10pm

‣ Akabanebashi station, exit C1

ukai.co.jp

Under the ever-watchful eye of Tokyo Tower, you'll find this tranquil tofu specialist restaurant housed in an impressive samurai-era merchant's house and cocooned in a beautiful garden. The house also contains one of Japan's oldest sake mills. Tofu Ukai is a labyrinth of 56 intimate rooms, all sparsely furnished with tatami mat floors. Each of the rooms overlooks lush grounds, the thatched roof of the grill hut, koi ponds and waterwheels. The wholesome and picturesque food is delectable and seasonal kaiseki cuisine (a traditional multi-course meal) is the star. They serve the freshest tofu imaginable, made on the premises in a 'tofu hut' (you'll see staff impeccably dressed in traditional uniforms as they make their way back and forth with fresh slabs of curd). Tofu sceptics will immediately be smitten, carried away by the presentation, precision flavours and historical setting. Lunch is the time to go if you are on a budget, or opt for dinner for a healthy indulgence in a truly atmospheric night setting. A memorable dining experience that promotes both inner health and inner peace.

FOODIE NOTE
T's Tan Tan also has a shop in Ueno and they have packaged ramen for sale in Duty Free at Haneda Airport. Perfect omiyage (regional souvenirs) for all your friends who prefer plant-based ramen.

T'S TAN TAN
ティーズタンタン

Tokyo Station

1-9-1 Gransta Tokyo Station, Marunouchi, Chiyoda-ku

Mon–Sun 10am–9.30pm

‣ Tokyo Station, Keiyo St area

ts-restaurant.jp

This vegan ramen joint in Tokyo Station (*see* p. xix) is a staple lunch or dinner stop for those looking for plant-based eating in the big city. T's Tan Tan is a boon for anyone who finds themselves craving the piquancy, umami profile and the satisfying slurp of ramen without the pork and everything. It offers a range of tasty soups on a budget, set in an unfussy room that allows you to dip in and out; it's true fast food with a mindful nod to not eating meat. Order on the tablet at your desk, choosing from a range of ramens enhanced with soy and sesame and stocked with perfectly chewy noodles and fistfuls of greens and bean shoots surrounding a generous soy meatball. Add vegetarian gyoza, soy meat and/or rice as a side for the perfect vegan power lunch before launching yourself back out into the Tokyo Station maelstrom.

Whether you are looking to seriously invest in retail therapy or just window shop for ideas and future purchases, Tokyo has it all. From monolithic retail hubs with world-class cafes, restaurants and galleries, ubiquitous megastores spruiking endless brands and labels, to quiet backstreets with small makers' stores who have been plying their trade for centuries.

The possibilities in Tokyo seem limitless and you'll have to exercise a little control. From whimsical, youthful fashion in Harajuku, to high-end spending in Ginza or Aoyama, sifting through homewares in Shinjuku and Shibuya department stores, or rifling through racks in vintage stores in Shimokitazawa or Koenji, the quality and variety are unrivalled and the spaces are truly spectacular.

A cache of up-to-the-minute fashion is on offer, although be mindful that Tokyo brands usually fit one size: extra small. Luckily, a stylish and quirky array of accessories, including bags, hats and scarves, will Tokyo-a-fy your home wardrobe.

Tokyo's shopping is known for manufactured toys and over-the-top electronics, but it also has centuries of perfection, producing hand-crafted specialties. Pharmacies spill onto the streets offering up the latest in skincare and cosmetic finds, and music stores are stuffed to the rafters with new releases and vintage vinyl. Craft and stationery stores offer a dazzling and dizzying array of art supplies, paper and journalling products — including custom-made for you.

There is something for everyone and Tokyo never disappoints, so dive headlong into the shopping vortex. Maybe just keep one eye on the credit card balance.

TOKYO SHOPPING

東京物語

RAGTAG
ラグタグ

Shibuya

1-17-7 Jinnan, Shibuya-Ku

Mon–Sun 11am–8pm

‣ Shibuya station, Hachiko exit

ragtag.jp

RAGTAG seek out, gather and upcycle designer clothing, then arrange it over four floors in their Jinan store in the relaxed backstreets of Shibuya. Upcycled contemporary fashion is relatively new to Japan and is gaining momentum with the country's eye on the circular economy. This phenomenon has proved a popular way for style-conscious Tokyo-ites to sell their season's old-brand pieces to a hungry market who can purchase high-end brands that would otherwise have out-of-reach price points. An enviable collection of pre-loved label clothes, shoes, jewellery and accessories await, so if you're looking for that special archive piece from COMME Des GARÇONS, Issey Miyake, Louis Vuitton or Maison Margiela, you've come to the right place. Japanese brands like United Arrows, Beams and HYKE are also represented, as are The North Face, Fred Perry, Acne Studios, A.P.C., and more. Each piece is in great vintage condition or loved back to life. Take your time to find that classic item that fits you to perfection (Japanese sizes can run small) and is effortlessly stylish. Don't miss RAGTAG's newly relocated sister store on breezy Cat St, a side step from the original and iconic Cat St location.

YAECA
ヤエカ

Ebisu

2-20-15 Ebisunami, Shibuya-ku

Mon–Wed & Thurs–Sun 12–8pm

‣ Ebisu station, east exit

yaeca.com

Understated fashion is something the Japanese seem to do effortlessly, and we can think of no better example of this than Yaeca, founded by Tetsuhiro Hattori and Kyoko Ide in 2002 with the express intention of combining subtlety and sophistication with versatility and a minimalist aesthetic. Guarded by a tangle of greenery, the tiny store in neighbourhood Ebisu is a haven for minimalist dressers. They make timeless pieces (we hesitate to call them basics) and you'll mostly find everyday wear like shirts, pants, dresses, coats and jackets made from natural fibres like cotton, wool and linen. In keeping with the straightforward philosophy, colours are neutral, and silhouettes are understated, but it's deceptive as the structure and detail instantly elevates the clothing, making your daily uniform seem effortlessly chic. Longevity is a key part of the Yaeca aesthetic, and although trends, styles and shapes come and go, like us you'll find yourself reaching for that Yaeca piece five, 10 or 15 years into the future. Also visit **Yaeca Apartment Store** in Nakameguro and **Yaeca Home Store** in Shirokanedai.

THE YARD
ザ・ヤード

Jingumae

3-36-26 Jingumae,
Shibuya-ku

Thurs–Mon 11am–7pm

› Gaiemmae station, exit 3

kimono-yamato.co.jp

A ladies and gents tailor in a store with a distinct minimalist dynamic, as well as a modern brand by the 100-year-old kimono company Yamato, The Yard is where you go for full kimono dress, or to buy separates as modern pieces to give your current outfit a Japanese twist. The Yard has made a name for itself as the contemporary frontier of the classical Japanese outfit and has become a stark counterpoint to Tokyo's current street and casual wear aesthetic. It deconstructs traditional dress for the 21st century sophisticate, effectively using the kimono to act as the classic 'white shirt.' Knowledgeable staff helped Michelle choose a yukata (summer kimono) which was then tailored to her size, ready at a later date for pick up. This is a wonderful entry point into the world of kimono as it is a more casual and affordable, and yet still refined, style of dress. Swoon over their range of haori jackets, obi and obidome (kimono sashes and accessories), zori sandals, tabi socks and bags. Kimono fabric is sold by 'the yard' and features naturally dyed handwoven textiles, warp and weft, yarn and weave, interwoven linen, cotton, silk and hemp all conspire to make The Yard an immersive experience.

DESIGN NOTE
Ask about The Yard's kimono dressing lessons, which are perfect for anyone wishing to uncover this intricate, almost ritualistic sartorial art.

COMME DES GARÇONS
コムデギャルソン

Aoyama

5-2-1 Minami-Aoyama, Minato-ku

Mon–Sun 11am–8pm

‣ Omotesando station, exit A5

comme-des-garcons.com

The flagship store for COMME des GARÇONS (which literally translates to 'like the boys') is a showroom that blurs the lines between women's and men's fashion, as well as between creativity and retail. Designer Rei Kawakubo, the founder of the label, sculpts tortured futurist kimonos, androgynous samurai jumpsuits and gothic lace party dresses that make the space feel more like a contemporary art gallery than a fashion store. A clientele with a taste for the edgy head here to see if they can carry off Kawakubo's intricately engineered creations. They'll never look as good as the staff though who float around the store like museum exhibits on an interstellar catwalk. If your budget doesn't stretch to a COMME dress or jacket, you can always pick up one of the olfactory Japan-only fragrances (Steve's all-time favourite is Incense Avignon), or one of their coveted PLAY heart T-shirts. The **COMME des GARÇONS Marunouchi store** has a wonderful polka-dot façade. It shares the space with **The Rose Bakery**, a relaxed cafe that does a healthy, vegetarian-friendly lunch.

FOG LINEN WORK
フォグリネンワーク

Shimokitazawa

5-35-1 Daita, Setagaya-ku

Mon–Fri 12–6pm

‣ Shimokitazawa station, west exit

foglinenwork.com

The philosophy at Fog Linen Work is simple. Owner Yumiko Sekine believes in creating and selling elevated fashion and products for daily use. After 30 years in the business, Sekine opened this stylish minimalist store which converts linen sourced from Lithuania into covetable dresses and aprons, as well as tea towels, bedding, coasters, cushions and more. All clothing and items come in tasteful earth tones, or the store's signature checks and stripes. You'll find put-together Shimokitazawa residents shopping here, looking for ways to add a touch of class to their wardrobes and homes. Make sure you plan your visit to Fog Linen Work as it is closed on weekends, which is almost unheard of in Tokyo. Your Tokyo itinerary should definitely include a mid-week jaunt to breezy, boho Shimokitazawa for some serious vintage clothing and record shopping.

DESIGN NOTE
MOONSTAR Jiyugaoka won a Good Design award in 2024 and the architects ARA and KONTE were commended for designing a community-minded space that hinted at the materiality of the shoes in the interior design — elements such as canvas shoji screens and rubber fixtures.

MOONSTAR
ムーンスター

Jiyugaoka

2-16-27 Jiyugaoka, Meguro-ku
Wed–Mon 11am–7pm
‣ Jiyugaoka station, main exit
moonstar.co.jp

MOONSTAR is a bespoke shoe company whose origins began in 1873 in Kurume (Kyushu) when split toe socks called tabi evolved into a shoe with a rubber soul called a 'Jika Tabi' during the Meiji period (1868–1912). Jump forward to 1925 when the company was inspired to make athletic footwear, resulting in a contemporary philosophy for a new kind of modern footwear for customers. Making their Tokyo home in Jiyugaoka, this community-minded neighbourhood fits the ethos of the brand down to the soles of their feet. Their 'shoes like pottery' are gender neutral with a classic silhouette, with echoes of a mid-century American gym shoe. However, their range diversifies, from loafers to boots to Mary Janes, with many designs and colours available for both adults and children. Made from the finest materials, they use a time-honed technique where the rubber is baked in a kiln – literally like pottery. This 'vulcanised' or ka-ryu technique produces comfortable shoes that are flexible, yet made to last. Although stocked in limited retailers around the city, MOONSTAR's flagship store in Jiyugaoka showcases many of their product lines.

TOKYO STYLE
東京スタイルワークウェア

WORKWEAR

As soon as we arrive in Tokyo, we buy the latest *Popeye* and *Brutus* magazines. Both of these pop-culture periodicals alerted us to an interesting phenomenon — workwear as a new hybrid fashion statement. Workwear's premium fabrics and expertly cut styles last the test of time, and the rugged clothing allows for a relaxed attitude. Sturdy hard-wearing fabrics are teamed with classic postwar Ametora or Amekaji (American casual/traditional) or European styles of work jackets, shirts and pants. Japanese construction worker 'Tobi pants' have made the leap from street to runway and can be found at classic workman stores (the finest example being **Toraichi** at 3-37 Higashikomatsugawa, Edogawa-ku). **The Real McCoys** (6-25-8 Jingumae, Shibuya-ku) is a one-stop shop for workers' jackets, rugged denim and pants and everything in-between. The **Visvim** store (2F, 5-10-1 Jingumae, Shibuya-ku) in GYRE (*see* p. 38) has an incredible interior with a giant shimenawa (sacred rope). It's a premium brand that features handmade silk denim. Brands like Danton and Nanamica draw inspiration from nautical themes. Japanese label **Danton** (6-12-17 Jingumae, Shibuya-ku) is known for its unisex quality and classic workwear silhouettes. **Nanamica**'s (26-13 Sarugakucho, Shibuya-ku) high-profile co-labs are coveted by collectors. All three brands should be on your list if you love a stripy top, a buttoned-down knit or classic wool peacoat. **Bshop** (1-1-5 Nishishinjuku, Shinjuku-ku), stocks many uniform and sailor-style brands if you want a good one-stop shop. **Okura** (20-11 Sarugakucho, Shibuya-ku) in Daikanyama sells chic fashion with silhouettes based on classic indigo dyed workwear and simple fashion; it's housed in a beautiful building based on a classic kura warehouse.

OUTDOOR WEAR

Is it haute couture on the peaks? Or intrepid exploration on the city streets? Either way, outdoor wear in Tokyo is a fashion statement in its own right and happily worn as regular attire. Function follows form, with sharp cuts in rugged long-lasting premium fabrics, making the urban Tokyo-ite feel ready for any test thrown at them in the great indoors. One of Japan's most beloved outdoor brands **Montbell** was founded in 1975 (2F, 3-1-1 Kyobashi, 1, Chuo-ku), and sums up this cross-genre of lifestyle and dressing perfectly. Founder and renowned climber Isamu Tatsuno is inspired by the Japanese tradition of kinobi; function is beauty, lightness is speed. Enjoy the **Snow Peak** (KITTE 4F, 2-7-2 Marunouchi, Chiyoda-ku) collection, a catwalk for camping, at the **KITTE** (*see* p. 34) store. Founded in the 1950s, Snow Peak's hiking and camping gear are almost too good to use and might look more suited to a date than out in nature where they could get scuffed or soaked. The stylish camping accessories will have you making open-air coffee and barbecuing in your backyard. Former Issey Miyake designers Keita Ikeuchi and Mihoko Mori's functional and stylish 'new' kid, **And Wander** (founded 2011, Shin-Tokyo Building, 3-3-1 Marunouchi, Chiyoda-ku) make everyday attire and outdoor wear that blur the lines between town and country. In the backstreets of Shibuya, **Nicetime Mountain Gallery**'s concept store (3-55-2 Hatagaya, Shibuya-ku) packs in a lot of Japan's best outdoor brands whilst celebrating the lifestyle within their gallery and cafe. Why not do some urban exploring of your own, and hunt out the brand's archive collections in vintage stores like **RAGTAG** (*see* p. 22).

DENIM

Hard-wearing Japanese denim is revered worldwide. It has been cut, worked, shaped and engineered into styles that have influenced fashion designers globally and changed the face of denim construction forever, moving it from workwear to everyday wear and even onto the catwalk. Tokyo is full of opportunities to level up your denim wardrobe and given most people wear jeans at some time, a trip to the capital on a denim buying mission will net you great finds in contemporary and vintage denim, be they Wrangler, Levi's, Lee or some other classic brand. Denim is an integral part of what the Japanese call Amekaji, a style of everyday wear that is inspired by American casual clothing.

For a one-stop shop head to Shimokita's **Bears'** (2-9-3 Kitazawa Setagaya-ku) who stock the finest purveyors of Japanese selvage denim (high quality/rare fibre) and rugged denim in light, mid and heavy weight varieties guaranteed to wear well and produce a good fade. Brands include Oni Denim, Samurai Jeans, Tanuki, Big John and Japan Blue Jeans.

If you think that your jeans are unsalvageable, think again: **The Denim Doctor** can be found instore at Bears' and will fix your denim disaster with some deft visible or invisible mending, depending on your preference.

MUJI
無印良品

Ginza

3-3-5 Ginza, Chuo-ku
Mon–Sun 11am–9pm
‣ Ginza station, exit B4
muji.com

A Japan stalwart, now ubiquitous around the world, **Muji** only stocks its own products and has an enormous range of elevated minimal, simple and clever basic clothing, accessories and homewares. Essentially a 'life brand,' Muji's graphics and product development are distinctly minimal, bordering on plain packaging but despite having an almost anti-design, they have won many design awards. You'll be familiar with the store, but seeing it on its home turf is something else entirely. The ranges are bigger and co-labs and brand specials more plentiful in Japan. The **Muji flagship** in Ginza has multiple floors of clothing and homewares and includes a hotel, **Muji Labo** and **Atelier Muji Ginza** (art gallery and books), fresh produce and bentos to go. Muji in Shibuya (Shibuya station, exit A6b) and Ueno (Ueno station, exit 4) include **Cafe&Meal Muji**. Satellite Muji stores include **Found Muji Aoyama** (Omotesando station, exit B2) for rustic and ethnic sourced homewares, and Muji in Daikanyama (Daikanyama station, central exit) has a large selection of **Muji Labo**, a clothing range with upscale fabrics and designs. Cult items to take home include Muji's packaged range of snacks and drinks (Steve loves the white chocolate covered freeze-dried strawberries).

LOFT
ロフト

Shibuya

Loft is a multi-level homewares and lifestyle retail store featuring quality Japanese products and a well-curated selection from around the world. Stationery fans will be in heaven with a range of washi tapes, washi papers and accessories and the kitchenware and cookware sections will have you planning a revamp of your kitchen cupboards. Seasonal showcases include small-maker produce and products and specialist items from regional Japan. This Loft flagship store is in Shibuya but a bigger multi-level store can be found in Ginza (Ginza-itchome station, exit 8).

21-1 Udagawacho, Shibuya-ku

Mon–Sun 11am–9pm

‣ Shibuya station, exit A3a

loft.co.jp

HANDS SHIBUYA
ハンズ

Shibuya

The 'one-stop creative shop' is how Hands describes itself, and the range of homewares, stationery and travel goods here will throw you headlong into a shopping vortex where any sense of time is quickly forgotten. There is plenty in-store to enhance your lifestyle, but Hands is really all about inspiring you to style up your kitchen, choose the perfect umbrella or camping gear, put together a sticker album or generally get involved in any DIY project you can think of. The expensive range caters for hobbyists, handy-men and -women and professionals alike. If you have ever wanted to do it yourself, your journey starts here. If you haven't, don't be surprised if you come out of Hands with a sudden passion for quilting or home renovation. All hobbies are catered for, from very big to very small. As Hands itself says, 'create your own life in your own way with what is available within reach.'

12-18 Udagawacho, Shibuya-ku

Mon–Sun 10am–9pm

‣ Shibuya station, Hachiko exit

info.hands.net

TRAVELLER'S NOTE

Loft sell an extensive range of travel bags and accessories, just in case you find yourself needing to check in an extra piece of luggage.

DIY NOTE

There are also large Hands stores in Shinjuku and Ginza, and various smaller outlets around the city.

DEPARTMENT STORES
デパート

Departos, as Tokyo's department stores are known, are curated shopping and retail therapy spaces teamed with culture, beautiful displays, elegant wrapping, delicious food options and art. Most departos have a lively basement floor selling freshly made food and packaged sweets. Many also have a top floor gallery with unbelievable exhibitions. Departo window displays are spectacular, and often contemporary artworks in themselves, vying for attention along the major thoroughfares.

Mitsukoshi (1-4-1 Nihonbashi, Chuo-ku) opened in 1673, selling chic kimono from a stall on the Nihonbashi Bridge. The current building, designed by Tamisuke Yokogawa, was completed in 1914. Sumptuously renovated in 1935, many of the luxurious interior statements remain today, making the departo feel like it has bottled history. Kengo Kuma's reimagining of the space in 2018 is a contemporary marvel. 'The White Forest' is as it sounds, an origami construction that fills the ground floor, turning into an elegant world of cut-out white trees. Add exemplary shopping, a fabulous food hall and a central galleria space with an 11m-high Magokoro Tennyo 'heavenly maiden' statue (Gengen Sato 1960), and lifts operated by white-gloved ladies, and you have one of the world's most memorable shopping experiences. It is also a famous Ginza meeting spot and 'I'll meet you at the lions' is an oft-spoken phrase in Ginza; as you'll see, a large pair of bronze lions, modelled on London's Trafalgar Square, guard the entrance to the store. Don't mix this store up with the newer version, which can be found in central Ginza.

Beginning as a kimono store in 1886, **Isetan** (3-14-1 Shinjuku, Shinjuku-ku) is a haven of sophistication in unkempt Shinjuku. The window displays are spectacular visual feasts that set you up for exceptional shopping. Spread over eight floors, you'll uncover stunning displays propping designer fashion, kimono and obi sashes in sumptuous fabrics and a generally more luxe take on the usual department store. The homewares section features an excellent selection of Japanese design, both traditional and contemporary. The real attraction however is the food hall, a mouth-watering culinary adventure where both Japanese and Western cuisine are represented. The sweets section is without doubt one of our favourite places to go in Tokyo. Head to the rooftop garden for an urban picnic in a surprisingly lush haven surrounded by Shinjuku's towering landscape.

Nihonbashi Takashimaya (2-4-1 Nihonbashi, Chuo-ku) is opulent and tasteful. The exterior, with its iconic red canopy covered windows creates an instant impression, and once inside, you'll be amazed by vaulted ceilings and ornate ironwork surrounding a central chandelier designed by Togo Murano, which hangs over an atrium dressed in marble. It even has its own shrine and a fountain on the 8th floor (and paradoxically the cute and contemporary **Pokémon Center DX** on the 5th floor). Takashimaya's elevators are a delight — the detailed ironwork, wood panels and gold-plated doors are stunning and have a traditional allure. Black-gloved attendants add a touch of charm that will make you feel like you have stepped back into a better, more considered time. The food hall is probably our favourite in Tokyo, and that is no mean feat given that we have a serious department store food hall fixation. Superb.

SHIBUYA PARCO
渋谷パルコ

Shibuya

15-1 Udagawacho, Shibuya-ku

Mon–Sun 10am–9pm

‣ Shibuya station, Hachiko exit

shibuya.parco.jp

Billed as the 'new face of retail', Shibuya Parco has re-opened to great fanfare after a much-lamented closure and tear down in 2016 of the 1973 classic. Luckily for devotees the aesthetic remains, a vigorously youthful multi-brand store dedicated to presenting the best of boutique Japanese and international fashion and accessory labels. The 'new face' comes in the form of several tech upgrades, including interactive walls – a new take on the department store info touchscreen, where visuals transform and mutate when you make contact. Luxe brands are on the ground floor, floors 1–5 feature the more cutting-edge brands and other floors play host to pop-up gardens, restaurants, cinemas, **Parco Museum** and **Gallery X by Parco**, and a fabulous 6th floor gaming zone, **Cyberspace Shibuya**, which features a **Pokémon** dream world. You'll also find an outlet for highly collectible brand **Pop Mart**, which sells 'blind boxes' with a surprise toy monster like a Zimomo or Labubu.

KITTE
キッテ

Marunouchi

2-7-2 Marunouchi, Chiyoda-ku

Shops 11am–8pm, restaurants 11am–10pm

‣ Tokyo Station, Marunouchi exit

marunouchi.jp-kitte.jp

Kengo Kuma completely refashioned the old Tokyo General Post Office in 2013 into KITTE, a contemporary shopping space with a soaring ceiling (perfect for impressive Christmas displays in December) and gallery style walkways that house some of Tokyo's most tasteful destination shopping. Long-serving incense brand **Kungyokudo** (*see* p. 14), sits alongside **Hokuroku Sousui**, a chic store specialising in simply presented, yet exquisite, soaps, handcreams and essential oils that utilise natural ingredients. **Nest Robe**, **Nop de Nod**, **CLASKA Gallery and Shop 'DO'** and **The Shop** have upscale and inventive Japan-only fashion. Likewise, homewares with an innovative edge can be found at **The Good Design Store**, **Angers Bureau** and **Nakagawa Masashichi**, while **Iori/Shin Ehime** has a range of comfy towels from **Imabari Towel** (*see* p. 57). **Snow Peak Land Station** (*see* p. 27) caters for your designer camping goods and clothes that you'll be happy to wear in both urban and rural settings. It even has a cafe with camping chairs and a curry menu. Don't miss the rooftop space which has spectacular views of the trains at Tokyo Station.

DINING NOTE
The Shibuya Parco basement features **Chaos Kitchen**, designed by Sosuke Fujimoto, a re-creation of a classic yokocho (alleyway). It hosts **Masaka**, a rare vegan izakaya (pub with small plate food), and features genderless toilets (in fact the floor is described as 'genderless').

HISTORY NOTE
KITTE also features a fascinating look into the past by displaying the preserved **Old Postmaster's Office**. KITTE is Japanese for postage stamp (see what they did there?), and conveniently, a large post office still operates on the ground floor.

FOODIE NOTE
The **CIBI Corner Store** in Kitasando is a lovely spot for a morning coffee and avocado on toast.

HIKARIE SHINQS
渋谷ヒカリエ

Shibuya

2-21-1 Shibuya, Shibuya-ku
Mon–Sun 10am–9pm,
‣ Shibuya station, east exit or exit B5
tokyu-dept.co.jp/shinqs

Hikarie ShinQs brings together Tokyo's best design retailers, galleries, cafes and restaurants in a concept department store over 11 floors. Stand out moments include **Margaret Howell**, **Urban Research** and **CLASKA** for up-to-date fashion; **Collex**, **Idee** and **Today's Special** for excellent everyday household items; and **Smith** for retro-inspired stationery. On the 8th floor you'll find **D&Department**'s design store and gallery, the **D47 Museum**, showcasing Japanese beauty and ingenuity in design and craft, both contemporary and traditional, with a fascinating regional focus that inspires you to explore the country in depth. After shopping, stop at **D47 Shokudo** for some home-style comfort food. Enjoy one of their regional sake tasting sets and some rustic fare while taking in stunning views of the Shibuya Scramble, Shibuya station and the area's gargantuan billboards. There are also excellent options for sit-down dining on the 6th and 7th floors and a selection of packaged food, wagashi (Japanese sweets) and various takeaway options on the basement levels.

CIBI TOKYO STORE
チビ東京店

Yanaka

3-37-11 Sendagi, Bunkyo-ku
Mon–Sun 8am–6pm
‣ Nippori station, exit 1
cibi.jp

Already a favourite in our hometown of Melbourne, the CIBI Tokyo Store has become our Japanese home-away-from-home. Owner's Meg and Zenta Tanaka's philosophy is simple. Their food, products and the warmth of their staff follow the philosophy of Head+Hands+Heart, referencing these three key Japanese elements (衣食住) for inspiration on ways to bring design, food and space to everyday life. Simple and delicious homespun meals put a smile on your face and practical and well-designed homewares put style into your home. Residing in a backstreet of the low-rise authentic neighbourhood of Yanaka, the store welcomes you through their sliding doors into a light-filled room with a soaring wooden beam ceiling where tables of locals and travellers are chatting happily over brunch. Meg and Zenta's personal history is blended through their food with Western flavours infusing traditional Japanese family recipes. The Japanese breakfast is a perfectly balanced and fortifying feast to help set up your day. Delicious lunch plates, sandwiches, muffins and cake pair perfectly with excellent coffee. Browse the range of own-brand condiments and daily tools, like **Sori Yanagi** glassware, **Masahiro Mori** plates, and **Noda Horo Amu** kettles.

GYRE
ジャイル

Omotesando

5-10-1 Jingumae, Shibuya-ku

Mon–Sun 11am–8pm

‣ Omotesando station, exit A1

gyre-omotesando.com

Residing at the perfect junction point of Cat Street and Omotesando-dori, GYRE (pronounced Gii-ray) is a collection of designer homewares, clothing stores, food stations and art in an angular sleek black box of a building designed by MVRDV architects. Perfectly curated up-to-the minute 'toys' for the house can be found at the **MoMA Design Store**, homewares with a mid-century modern bent at **HAY** on the basement level, and more upmarket designer items at adjacent shop **Cibone**. High-end fashion destinations like **COMME des GARÇONS PLAY**, and exhibition level clothing (in racks and cabinets inspired by the Victoria and Albert Museum in London) at **COMME des GARÇONS Trading Museum** make your shopping seem more like a visit to an art gallery. One of the highlights of GYRE is the **Uni** cafe and bar. The low-lit amphitheatre features an array of cascading wooden boxes, set at varying levels. Find a strategic place to perch, and sip your coffee while people watching. Food options also feature a cafe version of **Dandelion Chocolate** (*see* p. 116) and a breezy teppanyaki eatery, **Omotesando Ukai-Tei**.

PALACE AOYAMA
パレス青山

Aoyama

6-1-6 Minami-Aoyama, Minato-ku

Each business has its own opening hours

‣ Omotesando station, exit A5

Across the road from the **Nezu Museum** (*see* p. 69), is a retro-cool, late '60s condominium-style apartment building, Palace Aoyama, tenanted by some of Tokyo's most unique retail thinkers. **Arts&Science**'s aesthetic commandeers much of the retail space. Under the direction of former stylist Sonya Park, A&S has flourished since its inception in 2003. There is something about the way Sonya styles her spaces that makes us want to move straight in. **&Shop by Arts&Science** focuses on 'genderless and borderless' clothing and accessories. Everything from the wall treatments to the coat hangers are beguiling. Its cafe **Down the Stairs** has a simple menu focusing on beautifully prepared meals and snacks with quality ingredients paired with natural wines. Vegetarians, head there on Wednesday for their plant-based menu. **Over the Counter by Arts&Science** is a curation of domestic and everyday objects made by artisans from natural materials. Tea is elevated to an art form at **Arte Classica by Ishiguro Gallery**. Curated by Ishiguro Koichiro, this small but perfectly formed fine art gallery specialises in exceptional handmade chawan (matcha bowls). Non-conformist fashion designer **Takahiromiyashita The Soloist** has found an audience at Palace Aoyama too, with his hybrid street/Americana/rock & roll mash-up style.

CULTURE NOTE

Don't miss the **Eye of GYRE**, where they show small but excellent free exhibitions.

FOODIE NOTE

After you've strolled around the exquisite spaces, head to **Tempuraya Miyakawa** for Kansai-style tempura. The tiny establishment has been in business for over 50 years. It serves tempura with the perfect amount of batter and crispiness which earned owner Isao Kanemasa three Michelin stars.

TOKYO MIDTOWN
東京ミッドタウン

Roppongi

9-7-1 Akasaka, Minato-ku
Mon–Sun 11am–8pm
‣ Roppongi station, exit 8

Tokyo Midtown is a contemporary shopping centre featuring stylish retail-therapy, world-class art and a myriad of food options. There are excellent galleries on the premises including **Tokyo Midtown Design Hub**, **Fujifilm Square**, the wonderful **21_21 Design Sight** and **Suntory Museum of Art** (*see* p. 62), the latter being part of the Roppongi Art Triangle (*see* p. 62). Shopping highlights include **Nakagawa Masashichi Shoten**, the perfect store for Tokyo-centric gifts, small treasures or the perfect pair of socks or gloves. **Nihonbashi Kiya**, founded in 1792, is a gallery-like space that sells exquisite knives, cutlery and cookware. Handcrafted homewares can be found at **The Cover Nippon**. Flagship **212 Kitchen Store** has affordable yet exceptional everyday items. **Idée** is a chic lifestyle store with a breezy cafe. Visit the pocket-sized **Itoya** (*see* p. 53) for all your stationery needs. Food and drink highlights include **Toraya** for exquisite, jewel-like wagashi (Japanese sweets) and **Pâtisserie Sadaharu AOKI Paris** (*see* p. 121) for Frenchie sweets with a Japanese twist (try their matcha éclair or yuzu macaron). Break for lunch at popular fish-based eatery **Suzunami** or **Dashi-chazuke En**. Sake shop **Fukumitsuya** has excellent regional sake to take home.

LUNCH NOTE

We also sometimes like to lunch on the upstairs restaurant floor, where there are several exceptional options, both traditional and contemporary Japanese, as well as Western style.

OMIYAGE & SOUVENIRS
お土産

Tokyo has turned souvenirs into an art form, making it virtually mandatory (or at least very good manners) to return from a trip with something to delight loved ones. This has led to omiyage: exceptional regional souvenirs that come in a range of fabulous products, some simple, some expensive and detailed, and some emblematic of the place where they were bought. We've listed some of our favourites here, however one-stop shops like **Bingoya** (*see* p. 46), **Loft** (*see* p. 30) and stores on **Kappabashi-dori** (*see* p. xxxi), for example, have a vast range and offer easy access to some of the best. Michelle loves chocolate brand **RuRu Mary's** (Aoyama Kobayashi Building, 1-7-4 Shibuya, Shibuya-ku), which has award-winning packaging and 1933 elegance crossed with modern glamour; the chocolate sponge is exquisitely crafted making both the product and the package equally beguiling. **Tokyo Banana** (Tokyo Station, Tokyo Gift Palette, 1-9-1 Marunouchi, Chiyoda-ku), a flavoured sponge plumped with cream in a box with a pink bow, has become the number one omiyage associated with Tokyo; prepare to queue for regular flavour co-labs. The **maneki neko** (lucky cat) is also a popular gift, seen en masse at **Gotoku-ji temple** (*see* p. 180). The high-quality red-and-white cat dolls come in a range of sizes. We have one each, Blu-Tacked to the top of our computers to watch over us while we work.

DISORGANISED TRAVELLER'S NOTE

Tokyo Metropolitan Government's Tokyo BASE at Haneda Airport (Terminal 3, Edo Ko-ji store 31, F4, 2-6-5 Hanedakuko, Ota-ku) is your last-stop souvenir haven before you fly home.

DESIGN NOTE

Jump on the Rinkai line from Shin-Kiba station to Tokyo Teleport station to see the **Fuji Television Company building** (Kenzo Tange 1996), a delight for architecture and retro culture buffs, with their 'eyeball' branding reflected in the building.

CASICA
カシカ

Shinkiba

1-4-6 Shinkiba, Koto-ku

Tues–Sun 11am–6pm

› Shin-Kiba station, main exit

casica.tokyo

Hidden amongst the non-descript buildings in an off-grid bayside area, Casica is destination shopping that recalls an apothecary, library or museum, rather than a retail experience. Tanoshinal Inc. have masterfully created a design-driven universe out of vintage finds and artisan curation by displaying, hanging and propping all manner of objects, greenery and art. Enter via a rustic frontage into a thoughtful world of polished concrete, warm woods and vintage mismatched lighting. The first thing you'll notice is an indoor nursery that looks like a verdant Victorian parlour. Clever displays show a collection of new and vintage homewares and personal items, and at the back of the store you'll find a rustic modern furniture section, Japanese artisan objet d'art, global finds and a library featuring the store's favourite books. The cafe, **Arkhē Apothecary and Kitchen**, a space curated by Nanpu Shokudo, presents a small selection of healthy lunch options served on rustic ceramics. The wall of apothecary bottles signals the healing properties involved; each dish is made to fortify the immune system. Try the simple lunch tray of six healthy dishes or a medicinal herb curry, organic beer or herbal drink, served on large, shared tables overlooking the indoor jungle.

SOGETSU KAIKAN BUILDING
草月会館

Akasaka

Building 2F and 3F, 7-2-21 Akasaka, Minato-ku

Mon–Fri 10am–6pm, Sat 11am–5pm

‣ Aoyama-Itchome station, exit 4

sogetsu.or.jp

This is one of those spaces that couldn't fail to impress. On entry, you're immediately confronted by a superb **Isamu Noguchi** stone-tiered landscape, commissioned in 1977 when rockstar architect Kenzo Tange built Sogetsu. Climb up and stroll around the layered sculpture, immersing yourself in the accompanying eerie soundscape. Oki Sato's design firm Nendo Inc runs a coffee haven with serious architectural credentials on the 2nd and 3rd floor called **Connel Coffee**. The 2nd floor has a small cafe selling excellent brew coffee, which you can then take up to the next level, an impressive space which features a large polished floor, long wooden benches with stools, and tables with space-age swivel chairs, seating which recalls the building's '70s heritage. A long window overlooks Takahashi Korekiyo Memorial Park, which is also reflected in the cafe's many polished surfaces. The Sogetsu building is also host to **Ikebana Sogetsu**, started in 1927 by Sofu Teshigahara who wished to move away from the constraints of traditional ikebana (the art of flower arranging). Classes, run by ikebana masters, are held on the 4th floor and range from trial lessons to intermediate classes (with materials provided). If you're just passing through, it's worth popping into Akane Teshigahara's (the school's current headmaster) gallery.

CULTURE NOTE

Ikebana classes must be booked at least five days in advance through Sogetsu's website. Monday's international class is instructed in English. Japanese-speaking gents can book Friday's Men's Exclusive Class.

D&DEPARTMENT
ディーアンドデパートメント

Kuhonbutsu

8-3-2 Okusawa, Setagaya-ku

Fri–Mon 12–6pm

‣ Kuhonbutsu station, main exit

d-department.com

A short walk from Kuhonbutsu station or, if you're in the mood, a lovely stroll from Jiyugaoka, this flagship D&Department store is part cafe, part design shop and part vintage retail set in a converted '60s modernist warehouse. The store prides itself on showcasing the best in everyday objects by small makers and growers from all over Japan. Expect repurposed furniture and upcycled clothing alongside bottled soy milk, bags of rice and soybean crackers with packaging so exquisite you won't want to open it. The cafe has repurposed furniture, low-hanging warm lighting and plush armchairs from which you can enjoy a delicious curry or something from the seasonal menu. Coffee is made from beans roasted onsite and goes perfectly with the maple chiffon cake. D&Department also publish a top-notch travel magazine which you can browse through while kicking back with a craft beer. Check out their store, cafe and a small museum on the 8th floor of the Shibuya's Hikarie ShinQs building (*see* p. 37).

SPIRAL
スパイラル

Aoyama

5-6-23 Minami-Aoyama, Minato-ku

Mon–Sun 11am–7pm

‣ Omotesando station, exit B1

spiral.co.jp

Spiral is a design store, cafe, bar and gallery rolled into one. The snail-shell-shaped ramp of the gallery space gives Spiral its name and it is here that you'll find rotating exhibitions from emerging fashion designers, architects, furniture makers, jewellery makers and artists. The design store on the 2nd floor features a skilfully curated range of homewares which the store markets as 'simple products for everyday use'. You will certainly elevate your everyday life with beautifully crafted kitchenware, stationery, clothing, ribbons, jewellery and bathroom products. There is always a feature ceramicist, jeweller or other maker so you can pick up some handmade, one-off pieces as well. A lazy Sunday lunch in the downstairs cafe can set you up for more shopping on the 5th floor where you'll find minä perhonen's lifestyle store, **Call** and the **Sakurai Tea Experience** (*see* p. 143).

GALERIE DOUX DIMANCHE
ギャラリードゥディマンシュ

Jingumae

3-5-6 Jingumae, Shibuya-ku

Tues–Sun 12–6pm

‣ Omotesando station, exit A2

2dimanche.com

It's easy to see owner Hisashi Tokuyoshi's love of all things French and Scandinavian in this cosy craft oasis just minutes from manic Omotesando-dori. Make no mistake though, Galerie Doux Dimanche is very Japanese in its aesthetic. The delightfully twee interior is essentially a mini gallery with a design/craft store attached. Always dialling the kawaii (cute) factor up to 11, the gallery shows works by popular local illustrators, artists and makers (and some international ones; we were lucky enough to have a show there in 2019). The shop stocks a colourful selection of French-style bric-a-brac, fabric, stationery, and other items to add colour and warmth to your home. Look out for the gorgeous cards, prints and tote bags by Tokyo artist Yumi Kitagishi.

BINGOYA
備後屋

Shinjuku

10-6 Wakamatsu, Shinjuku-ku

Tues–Sun 10am–5.30pm

‣ Wakamatsu-Kawada station, Wakamatsu exit

bingoya.tokyo

Allow plenty of time to visit the five abundant floors of Bingoya – the perfect one-stop shop for Japanese crafts of all kinds. If you are on the hunt for noren (traditional fabric curtains), kimono, furoshiki (Japanese wrapping cloth), ceramics, lamps, fans, textiles and even furniture then you've come to the right place. The basement specialises in folk children's toys including Kokeshi dolls as well as clay and ironware. The 4th floor features upmarket lacquerware and traditional Japanese kitchenware buys. The rooms are small and replete with items, which reveal themselves as you climb up to each floor and move around the sectional space. Get yourself a basket and start stocking up; there are souvenirs and keepsakes aplenty in this expertly selected and curated haul which are both perfect for gifts and for you to expand your own collection of Japanalia.

CREATIVE NOTE

In addition to the gallery and shop, upstairs is home to an indie publisher **edition Paumes**, who write, curate and publish a range of inspirational, lifestyle books and zines that explore the environments of creative people globally.

CRAFT NOTE

Takumi Craft Shop (Ginza station, exit C3) showcases an extensive range of Japanese folk craft and artisan objects.

TRADITIONAL CRAFTS AOYAMA SQUARE
工芸青山スクエア

Akasaka

8-1-22 Akasaka, Minato-ku

Mon–Sun 11am–7pm

‣ Aoyama-Itchome station, exit 4

kougeihin.jp

If you're looking for a one-stop shop for traditional Japanese crafts, then this store run by DESAN on the broad stretch of Aoyama-dori has an extensive range. Since 1975 DESAN has promoted and fostered nearly 220 traditional craft industries in Japan and are affiliated with the Ministry of Economy, Trade and Industry. You'll find items from affordable furoshiki (cloth wrapping) to high-end lacquerware, sculpture and woodcraft. Beautify your home with Iwate ironware or Tochigi textiles and ceramics or specialised bamboo, pottery and glassware. Highly decorative Kagoshima Satsuma ware, Ehime washi paper and much more are placed delicately around the store like exhibits in a gallery. The wooden sculptures are museum-like pieces, as are the Kyo-Sensu fans from Kyoto prefecture. There are smaller, more playful items that still reflect their region of origin like papier-mâché daruma dolls and Kokeshi dolls, as well as an extensive range of crafting tools like calligraphy pens and ink slates. Check online for up-and-coming in-store exhibitions.

POPEYE CAMERA
ポパイカメラ

Jiyugaoka

2-10-2 Jiyugaoka, Meguro-ku

Mon–Tues & Thurs–Sun 12.15–7pm

‣ Jiyugaoka station, central exit

popeye.jp

At nearly 90 years of age, this tiny camera store has moved with the times, keeping one eye on advancements in camera technology while retaining an engaging vintage aesthetic and deep appreciation for the craft of photography. A DIY minilab, you can process your digital pics on the go here and then turn them into a creative masterpiece. It's perfect for professional photographers and those wanting to get a bit more hands-on with their happy snaps. The photo machines here take SD card and USB, or you can plug your camera or phone straight in. Choose from different paper stocks and sizes and then once you have your prints, pretty them up with the store's clever framing and mounting options. There are also stickers, stamps and tape if you want to decorate an album or portfolio. On our first visit to Popeye, we printed out our street snaps and made an album which we still take out and look over today, giving us all the nostalgic feels. Check out the alluring mix of new, antique, digital and analogue cameras while you're here and maybe even make that big purchase.

REPAIR NOTE

They also repair lacquerware at their 'craft clinic', so if you have a favourite piece that is broken and would like an expert to perform some delicate kintsugi (the art of visible repair), take it in with you. Consultations and quotes are free.

DESIGN NOTE

The Popakame Super TOY Camera is Popeye's well-priced, easy-to-use, own-brand camera that looks like a '70s rangefinder. It uses an original film called 'Popacolour 400' which can be developed in store!

WINGED WHEEL
ウイングド・ウィール

Harajuku

4-5-4 203 Jingumae, Shibuya-ku

Mon–Sun 10.30am–7pm

‣ Omotesando station, exit B1

haguruma.co.jp

Are you passionate about pen and ink? Are you into sending messages the old way and want to give your missive the personal touch? Head to Haguruma Co's Winged Wheel (admire the always inspiring window display) and roll out one of their sizeable drawers to see what paper treasures are inside. A third-generation family business, they have quietly been revolutionising the art and craft of stationery. Shelves of cards, boxes, notepaper, ribbons and other embellishments will give letter writers plenty of choice. The beautiful letterpress, bespoke invites and cards come in a surprising array of shapes and colours. Designs ranging from animals and flowers to traditional shapes and symbols all use paper of the highest craftsmanship. We love the #700 card range with animal and fruit motifs – revered symbols of luck, prosperity or beauty. There are plenty of exquisite items to choose from here, including a range of invitations you can have printed and personalised. Now all you have to do is plan a party and invite your friends! Or why not a wedding ...?

TRAVELER'S FACTORY
トラベラーズファクトリー

Nakameguro

3-13-10 Kamimeguro, Meguro-ku

Mon & Wed–Sun 12–8pm

‣ Nakameguro station, west exit

travelers-factory.com

Set up in 2006, Traveler's Factory is the home of Traveler's Notebook, a cult icon amongst the stationery obsessed. If you are into bullet-point journaling, or keeping a travel diary, buy the notebook, then customise it with a range of quirky and retro flavoured additions like slip covers, inserts and super-kawaii (cute) sticky labels with themes that include those cute characters the Moomins, Mount Fuji and more. The building, like your notebook, is pocket-sized, so once inside it is elbow-to-elbow journal junkies. Vintage-style stamps, pouches, covers, brass fountain pens, sharpeners, cases and even a range of lucky charms are all much-needed additions to your stationery village. Light rainwear (to shield your notebook from sudden downpours) is chic and folds neatly into your stylish Traveler's Factory tote bag.

PLEASE CHECK CONTENTS IMMEDIATELY
NAME
DATE
WAGES
SSP
イギリスの古い紙
ビンテージバスチケット
AROMATIC CASCARA
POISON
EPSOM SALT
ALCOHOL
Per Cent
АВТОБУС

DESIGN NOTE

Starting as an industrial washi tape company over 100 years ago (making products like sticky insect paper), it wasn't until 2008 when a trio of women started experimenting with the tape's creative boundaries that the new mt craft concept was born.

CRAFT NOTE

Snail mailers head to the 2nd floor where you can take your time writing a missive, purchase Itoya's limited-edition postage stamps and post from their cute in-house mailbox.

MT LAB.
エムティーラボ

Kuramae

3-14-5 Kotobuki, Taito-ku
Mon–Sun 10am–12pm & 1–7pm
› Kuramae station, exit 5
masking-tape.jp

Washi or masking tape obsessives and those who love to bullet journal make the pilgrimage here to be inspired. The perfect eco-friendly gift, mt's 'rice paper' tapes are treeless, biodegradable and use non-toxic glue. Sticking well, yet easily removed, and being thin but durable, are functional elements that make this little product perfect for crafters. Their low price point and pocket size adds to their take-home credentials. The mini mt lab. Kuramae store is a modest corridor with little in it but a long wall of mt tape in a dizzying array of colours, patterns and thicknesses, many of which are exclusive to the store. Their limited edition coveted co-labs and mt CASA (tape to decorate your walls) are just some of the reasons mt lab. is seen as a contemporary Tokyo design icon. It's likely that, as a collector of the tape, you'll get analysis paralysis as you admire the almost luminous wall of washi tape rolls. It's tape with personality and you can use it to wrap, adhere, bind and package up gifts, letters, parcels and pets (disclaimer: cats might not appreciate being covered in washi dots), elevating things from the everyday to the fabulous and adding a touch of Japanese artistry.

ITOYA
伊東屋

Ginza

2-7-15 Ginza, Chuo-ku
Mon–Sat 10am–8pm, Sun 10am–7pm
› Ginza station, exit A13
ito-ya.co.jp/ginza

Founded in 1904, this is Tokyo's pen-ultimate destination for anyone with an OSD (obsessive stationery disorder). Look out for Itoya's iconic red paperclip protruding from the building like a piece of modern art on busy Chuo-dori in Ginza. Its newly renovated tall and skinny architectural building almost looks like a ruler measuring up the skyscrapers on either side. Inside their two buildings you'll find 14 floors selling 'tools for work', with calligraphy pens next to high-tech pens, paper products of all shapes and sizes, beautiful origami paper, fans, fabric, cards and glue, all artfully chosen and arranged. Check out the selection of bags too, perfect to house your tablet or laptop. There are fun retro items as well, like the ever-popular yellow Fueki Doll Head corn starch glue and washi tape that comes in many varied patterns. A pop-up space, healthy juice bar and **Café Stylo** are all on site so you can pause to refuel while contemplating your healthy stationery obsession.

PIGMENT
ピグモントーキョー

Shinagawa

TERRADA Harbour One Building 1F,
2-5-5 Higashishinagawa, Shinagawa-ku

Tues–Sun 11am–7pm

‣ Tennozu Isle station, exit A

pigment.tokyo

Even getting to Pigment is an experience – take the short journey out to the bay on the cute monorail to discover the new store, designed by Kengo Kuma. Pigment caters to designers, professional artists and hobbyists with a staggering array of paint (estimated at over 4500 colours and textures) made from natural sources including minerals and types of soil, which are then enhanced using contemporary technology. The astounding vaulted bamboo ceiling reflects the store's philosophy of traditional methods being enhanced by modern innovation. The impressive array of paint colours looms large in a towering wall of paint pigment bottles, overwhelming in its scope. To accompany your paint selections, Pigment has over 600 types of brush and we were captivated by the wild bird, chicken and waterfowl feather brushes and the fluffy Nazebake (smoothing brush). There is also an extensive range of ink and paint slates, a wondrous display of washi paper and more. Thoroughly motivating for artists and aspiring creatives alike.

KAKIMORI
カキモリ

Kuramae

1-6-2 Misuji, Taito-ku

Tues–Sun 11am–6pm

‣ Kuramae station, exit A3

kakimori.com

Opened in 2010 in the crafty enclave of Kuramae, Kakimori is the kind of stationery store that stationery aficionados, writers and diarists go crazy for. If you are in the habit of writing down your experiences, scribbling poetry or jotting down poignant prose, Kakimori has all the tools to help you. Exquisite papers with an assortment of textures make it a tactile pleasure to create your masterwork. The unique selling point here is that you can assemble your own journals and notebooks from a range of paper, covers, spiral bindings and fasteners, according to your personal taste. The helpful staff will put together the parts of your book with deft skill while you wander around the store selecting from an extensive and colourful range of pens of all types including ballpoints and rollerballs that flow like ink and quill, and calligraphy pens with delicate, pinpoint tips. Tokyo is a city full of stories and, now, with the help of Kakimori, it's time to write yours.

CREATIVE NOTE

As with most art and craft stores, check Pigment's website for workshops and support.

CRAFT NOTE

The delightful wrapping paper specialty store **Regaro Papiro** is only a short walk away from Kakimori.

TOKYO POTTERY
東京で出会ううつわ

Ceramics in Japan are an elevation of the form. They can be unpolished and deliberately imperfect (embracing wabi-sabi), or they can be sophisticated, impeccable and impossibly elegant. Tokyo-ites embrace this and homewares stores gather majestic regional handcrafts to bring some flair to the city's homes. We try to buy a piece on every trip and each sits on a shelf in our home like a prized exhibit, or is used daily to add a refined visual aspect to meals; this appreciation of regional crafts has become a major part of our lives. They don't have to be expensive pieces, but we nearly always opt for handmade over manufactured.

Start by visiting **Utsuwa Kaede** (F1, 4-8-6 Jingumae, Shibuya-ku) in the Omotesando backstreets. The ceramics here have been given form by the elements, and wood, glass, earth and light filter into the homewares and small imperfections make these pieces unique and immaculate gifts and keepsakes. **Pejite** (5-6-9, Minami-Aoyama, Minato-ku), in a hidden lane in chic Aoyama, specialise in upscale handmade ceramics (and some distinctive furniture pieces and handforged wooden vessels) sourced from the Meiji, Taisho and early Showa periods, including pieces from Mashiko pottery town. The selections here are always sophisticated, tactile and surprisingly won't always break the budget. **Hakusan** (5-3-10 Minami-Aoyama, Minato-ku), in the '70s brutalist labyrinth of the Aoyama From-1st Building, has a selection of Hakusan and Sori Yanagi design ceramics that range from cute display items to impressive tableware. Visit them all and search out that special piece that speaks to you. Other unmissable pottery stores include **Utsuwa Marukaku** in Shinsen, **Kihara Tokyo** in Tomigaya, **Kiyo Ceramics** in Iidabashi and **At Kiln Aoyama** in Ebisu.

IMABARI TOWEL
今治タオル 南青山店

Aoyama

FROM-1st Building, 2F 203, 5-3-10 Minami-Aoyama, Minato-ku

Mon–Sun 10.30am–7pm

‣ Omotesando station, exit B1

imabari-towel.jp

Get 'knuckles deep' into the fluffiness of the towels, facecloths, socks and dressing gowns at Imabari Towel; all the towel products are made from cotton or bamboo and blended with the 'soft water' of the Imabari village on the island of Shikoku. The interior of the store is wall-to-wall blonde wood shelves, stacked high with colour- and pattern-coded towels. It's so artfully arranged it makes you wish you could get your bathroom redesigned (or at least cleaned and sorted) just like it. If you feel that your towel knowledge is lacking, check the website for the towel sommelier and learn all about the different types of towels, towel usage and how to find a towel to properly fit your needs. Your excessive towel knowledge will impress at dinner parties or random social engagements. Mostly though, you'll discover the towels that you have always been missing from your collection and with this in mind, we try to make sure that we restock whenever we are in Tokyo.

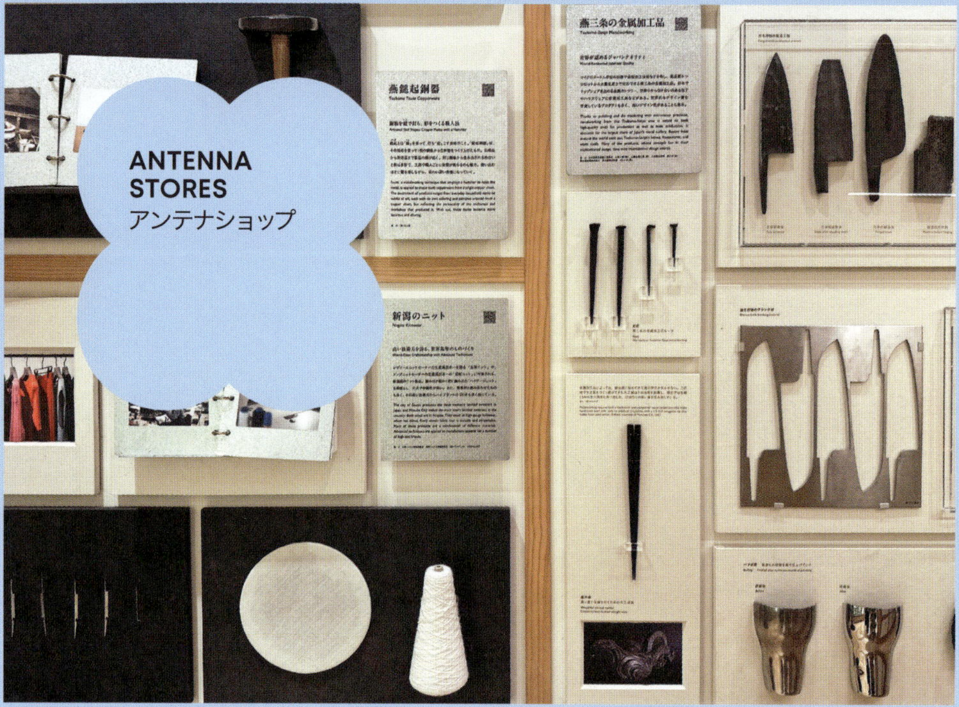

ANTENNA STORES
アンテナショップ

The act of gift giving when returning from different regions around Japan is a national pastime and has led to most towns having their own particular take-home presents, some food, some relating to a character or landmark. These are mostly only available in the regions or towns, but recently, small 'antenna' stores have popped up to celebrate the omiyage (regional souvenirs) and food specialties of various regions.

The neighbourhoods of Nihonbashi, Ginza and Yurakucho present many opportunities to delve into the specialties of islands like Hokkaido and Honshu. If you're in desperate need of black vinegar from Kagoshima, Toyama's soy sauce, Iwate's nambu tekki ironware or lacquerware from Ishikawa, you'll undoubtedly find a store in Tokyo to satisfy your regional curiosity. If a particular prefecture makes a dish or snack you crave, it's good to note that many antenna stores have fresh snacks, packaged delights or even restaurants that prepare the regional specialty.

Visit **Nihonbashi Toyamakan** (1-2-6 Nihonbashi Muromachi, Chuo-ku) for omiyage from Toyama. **Kagoshima Yurakukan** (1st to 3rd floors, Chiyoda building 1-6-4 Yurakucho, Chiyoda-ku) features south Kyushu's famous regional specialties, including tea and black pork. **Hyakumangoku Monogatari** showcases Kanazawa's omiyage, including gold-leaf, salt and Hyakuman mascot dolls. **Iwate Ginga Plaza** (5-15-1 Ginza, Chuo-shi) features specialties from Iwate prefecture and Morioka, including nambu tekki ironware and nambu senbei (crackers). Antenna Stores in Nihonbashi include Fukushima and Mie Prefecture. Ginza includes Fukui, Nagano and Niigata, amongst others.

DESIGN NOTE

Nearby tableware store **Proto** curate a sensitive range of ceramics and glass items.

SYURO
シュロ

Kuramae

1-16-5 Torigoe, Taito-ku

Mon–Wed & Fri–Sun 12–6pm

‣ Kuramae station, exit A3

syuro.shop

A favourite thing for us to do in Tokyo is to spend a lazy afternoon in Kuramae, always making SyuRo one of our first visits. SyuRo, which began in 1999, presents everyday items for living well, designed beautifully yet without flourish, that make any home an instant haven. At noon each day, SyuRo opens its large glass sliding doors to a clientele of thoughtful individuals who understand the importance of forever objects enhancing their lives. The voluminous warehouse space with a double-height ceiling is strung with industrial lighting and furnished with vintage wooden shelving which plays against white walls and concrete floors. Owner Masuko Unayama's interior design background shines with her selection of bags, wallets and earrings, room slippers and stoles made from natural cottons and linens. There are personal care products that use organic ingredients and are environmentally kind, such as organic towels, soft and cosy to the touch, teapots and cups, as well as stoneware and wooden plates and Avita glassware, Appi lacquerware and Workshop lacquerware. Their popular tin canisters form a patina and change in time with touch, warmth and moisture of the environment. SyuRo itself says, 'Ordinary things, modest ideas, and a big heart,' and this rustically beautiful store embodies those ideas.

At home, when we're dreaming up our next Japan trip, our thoughts always turn to gallery visits and the anticipation of what will be curated. We often book a trip around an exhibition or think of wandering through the vast gardens at Tokyo Metropolitan Teien Art Museum or sitting in the cafe at the Nezu Museum watching the shadows cast light in and around its origami-inspired roof.

Tokyo is a city with world-class art galleries and museums, with monumental architecture, often perfectly placed in verdant gardens or in sculpted cityscapes that defy the imagination. The city is a pre-eminent destination for any travellers wanting to explore how a culture adapts, evolves and ultimately becomes an unrivalled innovator in artistic pursuits and the creative arts.

Look out for Tokyo's creative use of architecture by making sure you are aware while walking around, looking up and down side streets and around corners to find examples of the level of thought and experimentation that shaped the city in postwar Tokyo.

TOKYO

東京物語

CREATIVE

ART TRIANGLE
六本木アート・トライアングル

With the completion of the **National Art Center** and the **Suntory Museum of Art** adding to the already established **Mori Art Museum**, the once slightly seedy Roppongi suddenly found itself as home to some of Japan's, and the world's, most spectacular art spaces. Further accented by the **21_21 Design Sight** (*see* p. 63), the **Fujifilm Square** and **Midtown's Design Hub**, Roppongi is now an unmissable art destination. The numerous galleries form a geographical shape in what is known as the **Roppongi Art Triangle**.

The **National Art Center** (Kisho Kurokawa, 2007) is a majestic, curved wall of glass and steel that has 10 galleries over three floors, playing host to constantly changing exhibitions, some which are free, all of which are memorable. The **Suntory Museum of Art** has themed exhibitions showing Japanese art and craft including kimono, ukiyo-e (Edo woodblock prints), silk-screen painting, tea ceremony utensils and ceramics. The rotating exhibitions take place in a moody space on the 3rd floor of Tokyo Midtown's chic retail hub. **Mori Art Museum** (Richard Gluckman, 2003), on the top of a sky-piercing tower with 54 floors, is devoted to national and international contemporary art. From the **Mori Art Museum sky deck**, large windows afford a panoramic display of Tokyo's extraordinary urban sprawl.

CREATIVE NOTE

Look out for street sculptures dotted around Roppongi. Kan Yasuda's 'ISHINKI (Shape of Mind)' sculpture is in front of Muji in Midtown and his 'MYOMU (Key to a Dream)' sculpture is in front of the Midtown entrance. Hinokicho park houses 'Fragment nº5' sculpture by Florian Claar, best viewed from the higher floors of Midtown. Walk under Roppongi Hills' Louise Bourgeois 'Maman' spider sculpture.

21_21 DESIGN SIGHT
トゥーワン・トゥーワン・デザインサイト

Roppongi

9-7-6 Akasaka, Minato-ku

Mon & Wed–Sun 10am–7pm

‣ Nogizaka station, exit 1

2121designsight.jp

Imagined into being by Issey Miyake with architecture by Tadao Ando, 21_21 Design Sight is a compact gallery on the grounds of Tokyo Midtown that hosts regular exhibitions that shine a light upon Japanese design. The building, a perfect intersection point between architecture and design, is a metal butterfly, squatting low into the grass, looking like it's about to take flight. Once inside, descending stairs open into a cavernous concrete bunker that shows an illuminating array of pop-culture exhibitions which explore motion and still graphics, industrial design, engineering and ingenuity. On our visits to Tokyo, we try to pop in to the space whenever we can to get up to date on design methodology or to marvel at the design history of famed Tokyo icons. On our visits we have seen fashion, music and culture in a variety of different forms from insects as models for design to the history of the Meiji Chocolate Company's design (including a giant replica and dissection of the popular chocolate mushroom) to the history and design of ramen culture.

THE JAPAN FOLK CRAFTS MUSEUM (MINGEIKAN)
日本民藝館

Meguro

4-3-33 Komaba, Megoro-ku

Tues–Sun 10am–5pm

› Komaba-Todaimae station, west exit

mingeikan.or.jp

Mingeikan is a museum dedicated to folk crafts, or should we say, everyday craft items – common crafts by unknown craftspeople. It was imagined in 1936 by the founder of the folk craft movement, Soetsu Yanagi and presided over by two famed ceramicists, Shoji Hamada and Kawai Kanjiro. In a quiet neighbourhood, Mingeikan is an essential visit for us and aligns with our passion for the concept that everyday items can and should be both beautiful and functional. The building itself (the main hall was designed by Soetsu Yanagi) features astounding traditional craft work with thick wooden beams and handrails, soaring and vaulted ceilings, and an impressive frontage, part of which was transported from Tochigi prefecture. Amongst the rotating exhibitions have been some of our all-time favourite Tokyo experiences. There's a palpable feeling of the tactile and the natural; you can sense the time, love and physicality that went into the various pieces on display. Expect targeted, expertly curated collections of ceramics, textiles, fashion, papier-mâché, bamboo objects, dyed fabric, paintings and more, all works which shun the high arts and lean towards objects for ceremony or everyday use and yet over time have become elevated treasures.

TOKYO METROPOLITAN TEIEN ART MUSEUM
東京都庭園美術館

Shirokanedai

5-21-9 Shirokanedai, Minato-ku

Mon–Sun 10am–6pm

› Meguro station, east exit

teien-art-museum.ne.jp

The former residence of Prince Asaka, this museum was reimagined and redesigned by French architect Henri Rapin. Completed in 1933, the exterior is chic European, the interior lavish Art Deco opulence, reflected in every doorknob, archway and fireplace. The ornate and finely detailed staircase, tiled floors and grates alone are worth a visit. Black-and-white check hallway tiles are straight out of a '60s French film or perhaps *Alice in Wonderland*. It's the perfect example of a building influenced by European styles but shaped by a Japanese aesthetic. The exhibitions always sit well in the space – painting, design, sculpture, furniture and decorative objects languish in airy rooms. The building sits proudly on vast expanses of manicured lawns with strategically placed modernist sculptures. In a surprise Japanese side garden, nooks and enclaves have ponds, water features, a teahouse, stepping-stones and bridges, all accented by exquisite planting.

DESIGN NOTE
Soetsu Yanagi is the father of famed 20th-century industrial designer Sori Yanagi.

CHRISTIAN CHURCHES
東京のキリスト教の教会

Tokyo's Christians commissioned some of the city's most innovative architecture in the 20th century. Materiality and light play key roles in Japanese church architecture, their look and feel both reverential and contemporary, built for a new generation of worshippers.

Saint Mary's Cathedral (Kenzo Tange, 1964; Edogawabashi station, exit 1A) was designed to reflect the concept of the lightness of a bird in flight. Tange's competition-winning design is one of Tokyo's boldest architectural statements, the concrete and aluminium exterior soars into the sky, a modernist metal arc standing stark against the city's skyline. A cavernous space houses Japan's biggest organ and presents an awe-inspiring vision of light shafts forming the shape of a cross.

The Harajuku Protestant Church (Ciel Rougle, 2006; Gaiemmae station, exit 3) stakes a bold claim on a quiet residential street. Its hard surfaces of concrete and metal are softened by fluid forms undulating across the frontage, designed to invoke music and spirituality. The interior also flows, an amorphous series of soaring organic arches. Six arches and a bell tower make up a symbolic number seven — representing the seven days of creation, seven notes in music, seven stars and the seven churches of Asia in the Bible book of Revelation. The space is an acoustic marvel.

The Anselm Catholic Meguro Church (Antonin Raymond, 1956; Meguro station, central exit) is located on Dorime (Fashion School) Street, and has flavours of mid-century Europe, with an eastern twist. Designed by one of the world's most notable brutalist architects, the church utilises a folded-plate construction of terracotta and concrete. Inside, the simple, understated interior is presided over by a heroic altar displaying a sculpted brass cross.

UENO PARK
上野公園

Ueno

Uenokoen, Taito-ku
Mon–Sun 5am–11pm
› Ueno station, park exit

Nature, museums, temples and world-class architecture, Ueno park has expansive grounds, is full of creative contrasts, and has an astounding amount to do. **The Tokyo National Museum** has the largest collection of traditional Japanese art in the city. **The National Museum of Western Art** (Le Corbusier, 1959) is a modernist masterpiece (*see* p. 71) with a collection to match. **The National Museum of Nature and Science** features a taxidermy of **Hachiko** the loyal dog (not creepy at all), and impressive exhibitions. Our favourite building on the Ueno park grounds is **Tokyo Bunka Kaikan** (Kunio Maekawa, 1961, *see* p. 71). The **Shitamachi Museum** explores life in Tokyo's poverty stricken but inventive downtown district in the early 1800s. **My sky hole 85-2: light and shadow** (Bukichi Inoue, 1985) entices you into the **Tokyo Metropolitan Art Museum**. **Ueno Zoo** features adorable pandas, a spectacular pagoda from 1631 and a teahouse. **Kaneiji temple**, **Kiyomizu Kannon Bentendo** (featuring a famous view through a circular tree branch) and **Toshogu shrine**, are just a few of the other treasures to be found. The park comes alive in season (*see* p. 187): autumn for ginko and maple viewing, and during hanami (cherry blossom season) when couples ride swan boats on Shinobazu Pond.

TRAVELLER'S NOTE

If you are visiting in hanami (cherry blossom season), **Aoyama Cemetery**'s breathtaking grounds is only a short walk away from the Nezu Museum.

DESIGN NOTE

The 2019 refurbishment of MOT saw signage designed by architect and interiors expert Jo Nagasaka whose materiality favours wood as a nod to Kiba park.

NEZU MUSEUM
根津美術館

Aoyama

6-5-1 Minami-Aoyama, Minto-ku

Mon–Sun 10am–5pm

‣ Omotesando station, exit A5

nezu-muse.or.jp

Early 20th-century philanthropist, politician and president of the Tobu Railway Company, Kaichiro Nezu was an avid practitioner of the tea ceremony and a collector of pre-modern Japanese and East Asian Art. In his memory, a museum on the family grounds was made, overseen by his son to honour his late father. The original was built on the grounds of the Nezu family residence in 1940–41; architect Kengo Kuma later reconstructed the museum after World War II. Inside, calligraphy, scrolls, paintings, textiles and time-worn Asian objects feature in the exhibitions and permanent collection. On the Nezu grounds you'll find one of Tokyo's most beautiful gardens which plays host to four historical teahouses secluded amongst the foliage, where women dressed in traditional kimono are often seen taking tea. Stroll the serene grounds floating over bridges and admiring lily pad–covered ponds. Plantings of irises, maples and bamboo complete the picturesque scene. Don't miss the contemporary **NEZUCAFÉ** nestled within the grounds which serves lunch sets, cake and tea, enjoyed with garden views through the glass walls, while the garden's silhouetted shapes flutter on the washi paper ceiling.

MOT
東京都現代美術館

Kiyosumi Shirakawa

4-4-1 Miyoshi, Koto-ku

Tues–Sun 10am–6pm

‣ Kiyosumi Shirakawa station, exit B2

mot-art-museum.jp

Kiyosumi Shirakawa is an area less visited by most, and yet it is one of Tokyo's up-and-coming enclaves and a hub for new coffee houses, smaller maker shops and bookstores. Sitting like a megalithic presence in the middle of this area, Museum of Contemporary Art (MOT), is one of our favourite Tokyo museums. Situated in Kiba park, the building alone is worth the visit – an iconic structure built in the 1990s that was refurbished and reopened in 2019, a steel and concrete, angular bunker that gives the appearance of a metal bug about to walk menacingly down the main street. Some of the curated installations and exhibits that we've seen at MOT have been 'life highlights', each expertly detailed, surprising and thoughtfully positioned in rooms, courtyards and spaces. The 'collection ongoing' is excellent, featuring 100 works on rotation chosen from an astounding 5000 works in their possession. Key works range from Warhol to Hockney and Lichtenstein and Japanese icons like Yoko Ono and Kohei Nawa. Make a day of it and lunch at the elegant **100 Spoons** or the more casual **Café & Lounge Sandwich Upstairs**. Or take a picnic and lunch in **Kiba park**. Museum shop **NADiff contemporary** has a fantastic array of art books and design objects.

METABOLISM & MODERNISM
メタボリズムとモダニズム

Postwar Japanese architecture was a patchwork of ideas, where architects became theorists and their work became mirrors to reflect the shattered yet resilient society. With strides being made in technology and materiality, architects wanted their buildings to have life, to appear to literally live and breathe; buildings that were bold structures in an evolving landscape. Metabolism was the most challenging and intellectual of these ideas. Incorporating elements of European brutalism but viewing their buildings as organic entities that lived and breathed within the environment, architects like Kisho Kurokawa and Kiyonori Kikutake founded Metabolism as a concept that buildings could represent societal change. These architects set about constructing buildings that could adapt like a living organism to external factors such as population growth, technology and environmental and societal shifts. Metabolism often utilised modules and pods, moveable and replaceable parts — ideas that we take for granted today but were new and innovative in the second half of the 20th century.

The late lamented **Nakagin Capsule Tower** (Kisho Kurokawa, 1972) was a fine example of this, and when it was deconstructed, separate capsule rooms from the hotel were displayed in shopping centres and galleries across Japan. Ginza's **Shizuoka Press and Broadcasting Center** (Kenzo Tange, 1967; Shinbashi station, exit 1), considered to be the first Metabolic building, is a central column sprouting 13 asymmetrical pod offices. Meant to adapt to demand for more office space, the building remains unchanged, with no pods added since construction. Despite this, it remains a realisation of Metabolism's core principals.

Modernism in Tokyo took on many forms leading to inventive and eye-catching constructions, many of which remain today. While exploring the Azabu-Juban area you'll likely come across the **Reiyukai Shakaden Temple** (Takenaka Corporation, 1975; Kamiyacho station, exit 2). A monolithic, oddball temple, this unusual Buddhist place of worship looks like a dwelling Darth Vader would reside in, especially if you happen upon it at night. Sometimes it is even referred to as the Spaceship Temple and it looks for all the world like a samurai-hat-shaped flying saucer that has landed and lowered its 'drawbridge' revealing myriad steps leading up into the building. Don't miss your chance to see one of architecture master Le Corbusier's Asian buildings (he only did two), the beautiful **National Museum of Western Art** (Le Corbusier, 1959; Ueno station, park exit) in Ueno park (*see* p. 67). The monumental reinforced concrete icon with floor-to-ceiling windows under a modernist block is a mid-century must-see and is now listed as UNESCO World Heritage. Next door is the **Tokyo Bunka Kaikan** (Kunio Maekawa, 1961; Ueno station, park exit) designed by one of Le Corbusier's apprentices. Both are a masterclass in postwar modernism. **Tokyo Bunka Kaikan** was Japan's first concert hall and it always impresses us with its sloped roof and modern American-meets-eastern feel. The building is a jumble of elegant shapes put together in a deliberately methodical and surprisingly new manner.

Our trips to Japan start months before we board the plane. The conversation that fills our home is centred around favourite dishes and eateries that we return to again and again. Japanese cuisine is different from any other – featuring subtle flavours, elaborate and elegant presentation, and the use of fresh, seasonal ingredients. Rice is a staple ingredient, and is served alongside dishes like tempura and tonkatsu (breadcrumb pork), as well as being a major ingredient in sushi. Sashimi (thinly sliced raw fish) highlights high-quality fish with minimal seasoning. Ramen, tempura, tofu, tonkatsu and yakitori, are all delicious choices too. All are enhanced by the umami profile, which includes salty, sweet, sour and bitter, brought to fruition with the use of soy sauce, miso and mirin (rice wine). Desserts like mochi (sweet rice cakes) and matcha-flavoured treats have a gentle sweetness.

As Tokyo has become more popular, queues now snake around the block, especially for businesses highlighted online or on social media. Your time may be better spent hunting out your favourite hole-in-the-wall or off-the-grid find for lunch or dinner. Small venues will most likely be full if you turn up without a reservation. It's important to note that lunch has strict service times of around 11.30am to 2pm (last orders at 1.30pm). Shopping centres and concept stores always have excellent food options, most with all-day menus, and departo food halls are great for picnic supplies. Yokochos (alleyways) are a great food night out as there are multiple venues serving up local fare with the drinks flowing. It can sometimes be difficult to find plant-based options in a city where bonito (a type of fish) is in many stocks and vegetable or tofu dishes. Konbini (convenience stores) and food halls can be your best friend with many delicious plant-based options available. Izakaya (small pub) eating can offer tofu dishes, salads and other veggie delights.

Japanese food is more than a cuisine – it's a history lesson in food, a map of agrarian dedication and, as proven time and time again, one of the healthiest diets on the planet. With a seemingly endless list of options, there's no doubt that food is one of the main reasons to travel to Tokyo.

TOKYO TASTEBUDS

東京物語

RAMEN

ラーメン

Ramen is renowned, a dish consisting of noodles in broth with various toppings and flavourings. From Chinese origins, the Japanese have shaped this simple noodle soup and turned it into an obsession for both locals and visitors. A staple meal for the worker, but sought out by the gourmand, it wouldn't be a stretch to say that ramen actually helps to fuel the frenetic energy of Tokyo. The dish is both complex and simple, diverse and comforting. Intense flavours are gained by boiling stock, nearly always with pork, and adding pork slices (although some excellent vegetarian options are beginning to surface). Soba buckwheat noodles can be thick or thin, depending on your choice. Tokyo is best known for a shoyu ramen tonkotsu (pork broth), where the broth is accented by soy sauce. Additives can include nori (seaweed), bamboo shoots, bean shoots, egg and green onions, amongst other things. Ramen is the very definition of umami and you can't go to Tokyo without trying at least one type of ramen.

EXPECT

- A queue for the most beloved shops.
- A small shop, some only have a few seats or standing only.

PRICE

- Always cheap.

POPULAR WITH ...

- Salarymen, students, visitors, everyone.

Types

Tonkotsu (pork broth), shio (salt), shoyu (soy sauce), miso, tsukemen (noodles are separate to the broth), abura soba (cold noodles and dipping sauce), hiyashi or reimen (chilled noodle dish), tantanmen (ground pork and sesame), niboshi (small fish ramen), kimchi ramen (with Korean pickled nappa cabbage) and negi ramen (spring onions). New variations are popping up all the time and creamy chicken broth ramen (tori paitan), light yuzu broth ramen and vegetarian ramen with broths like sesame and soy milk can be found.

How to order

Order from a machine at the front of the shop. It might be in English, it might have pictures (hopefully). Put money in, choose food by pressing buttons, get a ticket and give it to a person behind the counter.

Why we love it

Cheap, fortifying, satisfying, fast. Ramen shops excel in broth, chewy noodles, noodle thickness, and extras like egg, seaweed or menma (bamboo shoots). Side dishes like karaage (fried chicken) or gyoza can be just a few yen more.

You must try ...

Get in and out quickly so everyone can enjoy their bowl. Try as many varieties as possible. Slurp the noodles (it cools down the broth). Buy pre-packaged instant ramen to take home.

Have with ...

Beer.

Dine at ...

- Nakiriyu, Minamiotsuka.
- Sasaki Seimenjo, Nishi-Ogikita.
- Ramenya Toy Box, Higashi-Nippori.

GINZA KAGARI

銀座篝本店

The long queue permanently snaking outside this soba ramen eatery is your first clue that your tastebuds are in for a treat. Make sure you join the queue for ordering before joining the second queue to get in – scan the QR code and you'll be alerted when there is a seat for you. The minimal interior belies its status as a Michelin-star-rated establishment with a to-die-for silky rich creamy chicken ramen. The tori paitan (chicken broth) is a boon for the non-red meat eater. Soba noodles are firm and chewy perfection and the tender chicken slices delicate and flavourful. Slightly less traditional flavours like the chicken broth soy sauce truffle ramen beg to be explored. Add kick to your ramen with the miso 'pungency widening'. It widens the pungency.

Ginza station, exit B6/B7

RAMEN TENJINSHITA DAIKI

らーめん天神下 大喜

Tenjinshita's tasty ramen is a contrast to the many junk food joints in Akihabara. It's still fast food, but the ramen is better for you and will easily fill the gap of something to eat quickly while mid collectible, electronic gadget or manga hunting. Tenjinshita Daiki specialises in the Tokyo classic: shoyu ramen, a soy-based soup topped with chashu pork. You get a choice here however as there are two chicken-based broths, one light and one heavy and creamy (a big tick from Steve). You can also order a tsukumen – where noodles are separate from the broth and you'll totally feel like a local. Join the perpetual queue and find your favourite and see why this ramen eatery makes some serious noise in Akihabara (mainly slurping).

Akihabara station, exit Showa-dori

AYAGAWA RAMEN

手打 親鶏中華そば綾川

In an enclave in the breezy Ebisu backstreets, with **Bar Martha** (*see* p. 158) and **Tea Gate Coffee** just across the road, line up with locals in hip trainers (and a smattering of salarymen who haven't updated their suits), to enjoy some tasty ramen with a lighter touch. We recommend the chicken stock ramen. The umami piquancy of the gentler, creamier chicken broth is perfect. It arrives in ceramic pots on trivets delivered by a youthful staff who soundtrack the tiny 13-seat eatery with sugary chart pop. Don't skimp – order the chicken thigh on the side, some rice and perhaps one of their mountainous bowls of bonito (fish) if you're game.

Ebisu station, east exit

TOKYO STATION RAMEN ALLEY

東京ラーメンストリート

Amongst the most famous locations in the multi-layered Tokyo station is Ramen Alley, a busy enclave designed to mimic the atmosphere of a traditional ramen street. If you think station eateries are inferior in quality, think again. Ramen Alley is a selection of Japan's best-known ramen eateries, and the perfect place to indulge in ramen tourism. Join a queue and place your order at the machine (pictures and English instructions are provided). For creamy, rich pork broth tsukumen, try **Rokurinsha**. **Oreshiki-jun** and **Ramen Gyoku** are known for their unctious tori paitan (creamy chicken broth ramen). **Soranoiro** makes a delicious vegetarian ramen (the bamboo noodle version is popular). For a vegan option, head out of Ramen Street and follow the signs to the Keiyo line for **T's Tan Tan** (*see* p. 19).

First Avenue, Tokyo Station

TRAVELLER'S NOTE

If you are waiting at Narita bemoaning the loss of your beloved ramen, don't despair — there is a **Ginza Kagari** at the airport.

SUSHI AND SASHIMI
寿司と刺身

Sushi and sashimi are quintessential Japanese cuisine and Tokyo is famous for taking them to the next level. Pillows of lightly vinegared rice topped with fresh raw fish, or thinly sliced raw fish dipped in soy can be found in eateries that go from affordable to eye-wateringly expensive, depending on reputation and quality. The Western appreciation for these delicate morsels has grown steadily over the years and most people now make sushi and sashimi one of their must-go-to meals on every Tokyo trip. From markets and small conveyor-belt sushi joints to high-end dining and Michelin-star restaurants, melt-in-your mouth sushi (and accompanying rite-of-passage toppings like sea urchin roe), and sashimi, make for memorable feasts, and are also perfectly portable for picnics.

EXPECT

- A queue for many popular sushi eateries.
- High prices in famous sushi restaurants.
- Immaculate quality in high-priced sushi restaurants.

PRICE

- From reasonable to very high.

POPULAR WITH ...

- Locals and visitors, gourmands, students.

Types

Nigiri sushi (the classic rice topped with a variety of seafood), maki (sushi rolls), inari (sweet rice in pockets of tofu skin), temaki (cone-shaped hand-held rolls), oshi (pressed sushi) and temari (ball-shaped sushi). The most common types of sashimi are tuna, belly fat, salmon, prawn, amberjack, horse mackerel, squid, flounder and eel. A sashimi rice bowl is also a delicious option.

How to order

If you are in a high-end sushi restaurant, ask for the omakase (chef's choice) or there may be a set a la carte menu. At cheaper sushi restaurants, you sit at the counter and put your orders into the machine and it will be whisked to your table on small carts. If it is a conveyor-belt restaurant, take sushi off the conveyor belt as it goes around.

Why we love it

Sushi can be for high-end slow dining or for fast meals, or good for bento boxes and picnics.

You must try ...

As many varieties as possible. Don't be afraid of the ikura (salmon roe), unagi (eel) or uni (sea urchin roe).

Have with ...

Beer or sake. Eat a small piece of ginger between each sushi as a palate cleanser. Dip the sushi fish side down in soy.

Dine at ...

- Hirō Ishizaka, Hiroo.
- Uobei, Shibuya.
- Sushi no Midori, Shibuya.
- Matsue, Shibuya.
- Ginza Kyubey, Ginza.
- Hatsume Sushi, Ebisu.
- Hibi Hare Bare, Shinjuku.
- Sushi No Midori, Ginza.
- Sushi Dai, Tsukiji.

SUSHI AOKI
鮨青木

One of the most respected (and expensive) sushi restaurants in Tokyo, Aoki prides itself on the freshest fish served at the perfect temperature. Most people in the tiny room sit at the counter and watch the itamae (master sushi chefs) do their thing, expertly carving gleaming fish and laying it on pillows of sushi rice and presenting a memorable feast of sushi delicacies. Request the omakase (chef's choice) to find out what the chef considers to be the best dishes of the day, which will usually include sea urchin roe. Recommended are the omakase lunch sets, a good (and much less expensive) way to experience Aoki's perfectly crafted selection. Oh, did we mention that it has a Michelin star?

Ginza station, exit A2

ITADORI BEKKAN
築地虎杖別館

There are a plethora of sushi and sashimi eateries in the Tsukiji Outer Market (*see* p. 94), and it wouldn't be crazy to spend a large part of your time in Tokyo (and income) tasting everything they have to offer. If you want to add a touch of elegance and mystery (and sea urchin), slip down the dark, narrow alley and join the queue at Itadori Bekkan. Stools surround a large wooden counter, a tiny patch of the market where the day's freshest catch is expertly carved into the most delicate, melt-in-the-mouth sushi and sashimi. Fresh fish can be tried in an ascending scale of prices, depending on your budget. Most of the selections will feature Bekkan's famous uni (sea urchin) sushi.

Tsukiji station, exit 1

JAPANESE BREAKFAST
日本の朝食

As the old saying goes, 'eat breakfast like a king, lunch like a prince, and dinner like a pauper', and if you have adopted this as your mantra, then Tokyo is your happy place. The most fortifying start to the day, a Japanese breakfast includes all the food groups, and always seems too large to eat, yet leaves you feeling gently satisfied. The traditional Japanese breakfast originated in Old Tokyo in the Edo period (1603—1867) as a way to fuel citizens and give them ample energy for work. It's the perfect set up for the day's sanpo (stroll) around the capital. A ritual for us when travelling to Japan, we look forward to the variety of dishes and the ceramics used to serve each dish (the perfect blending of patterns and materials). Steve's sage advice is this: you can tell how good your Japanese breakfast will be by the quality of the miso. Michelle's tip: why not plug US indie pop band Japanese Breakfast into your headphones to get you ready? Miso soup, steamed rice, tofu, grilled fish (usually mackerel or salmon), an egg (either raw, onsen egg, soy egg or boiled egg), pickled vegetables, and either nori sheets, natto (fermented soybeans), a small salad, boiled vegetables or another vegetable dish of the proprietor's choice make up this sumptuous yet virtuous morning feast. Your hotel may make a traditional breakfast and if you are staying in a ryokan (traditional inn), they definitely will. Be sure to skip your usual Western fare and partake in this Edo period classic.

THE INTERNATIONAL HOUSE OF JAPAN
5-11-16 Roppongi, Minato-ku
Breakfast Mon–Sun 7–11am
‣ Azabu-juban station, exit 7 Toei Oedo line, or exit 4 Namboku line
i-house.or.jp

YAESU HATSUFUJI
Yaesu Underground Mall North 1, Yaesu 2-1, Chuo-ku
Breakfast Mon–Sun 7–11am
‣ Tokyo Station, Yaesu central exit
hatsufuji.com/yaesu

ONIGILY CAFE
An onigiri (riceball) breakfast for those who want an express version of a Japanese breakfast.
3-1-4 Nakameguro, Meguro-ku
Breakfast Mon–Sun 9–11am
‣ Nakameguro station, east exit 1
onigily.com

Also try these favourites ...
Hagiso (*see* p. 107) and **Cibi** (*see* p. 37).

SOBA
蕎麦

Soba is a popular noodle that appears in many of our favourite dishes. These traditional buckwheat flour noodles are famous for their nutty flavour and gently chewy texture. Served either hot or cold, soba is a versatile noodle. When served cold, soba often comes with a dipping sauce called tsuyu. Soba in hot broth is also a Tokyo staple. Rich in protein, fibre, and antioxidants, soba is definitely heathy. In Japan, soba noodles are eaten on New Year's Eve as a symbol of longevity and good fortune.

EXPECT

- Perfect, chewy noodles.
- Tasty broth or dipping sauce.

PRICE

- Usually inexpensive.

POPULAR WITH ...

- Locals and visitors, students, noodle lovers.

Types

Kake (with hot broth poured over), tanuki (with tempura crumbs), kitsune (with fried tofu), zaru (cold noodles and dipping sauce), sansai (with mountain vegetables like mushrooms, bracken, ferns and bamboo), toshikoshi (New Year's Eve noodles).

How to order

Sometimes there will be machines, sometimes not. Nothing too tricky about this one, just choose your noodles and enjoy.

Why we love it

Soba is a Tokyo staple, and very versatile. It can be a quick meal or elaborate dinner and appears in a range of dishes.

You must try ...

The cold soba and dipping sauce in summer with thick and thin soba noodles, a fast-track way to become a true Tokyo-ite.

Have with ...

A sake or a shochu (distilled spirit).

Enjoy soba cold with dipping sauce or in hot broth. Have an extra with your noodles, usually tempura or duck. Drink the soba water afterwards (sometimes shochu is added to this).

Dine at ...

- Nezu Soshian, Nezu.
- Kanda Matsuya, Kanda.
- Kanda Yabu Soba, Kanda.
- Toranomon Sunaba Soba (*see* p. 87).
- Dosanjin, Nakameguro.
- Soba Yakko, Meguro.
- Hirayama, Asakusa.
- Ittoan, Higashijujo.
- Soba Tajima, Nishiazabu.

DASHIN SOAN SOBA

打心蕎庵

We'll resist the urge to say 'dash-in' to this restaurant, but it seems appropriate as the flavour profile and perfectly chewy noodles at Dashin are sublime. A short walk from Shimokitazawa station will bring you to a chic entryway with yellow noren (traditional curtains) that part to reveal a restaurant that has perfected the noodle. Enjoy classic chilled soba with dipping sauce (zaru soba) or in a piquant piping-hot broth. Steve's pick was the kamo (duck) soba: tender slices of duck in a golden soup accented with yuzu lemon and accompanied by buckwheat noodles. As with all good soba, the staff will bring you the cooking water to drink, a cloudy nourishing broth.

Shimokitazawa station, south exit

ITASOBA KAORIYA

板蕎麦 香り家

You could be forgiven for thinking that you had walked into a pricey establishment at Itasoba Kaoriya, such is the architectural elegance of the interior which is chic and modern, with dark warm woods and low lighting. However, the price point is surprising for such quality fare. You'll get a choice of thin or thick noodles that arrive in a rectangular wooden box accompanied by a dipping sauce, pickles and rice. Choose from crispy tempura, tender duck and leek or a vegetable selection with gomodare, a sesame flavoured sauce. Extras include an exceptional tamagoyaki (omelette) and a flavoured rice. Pair it with a triple sake tasting set!

Ebisu station, east exit

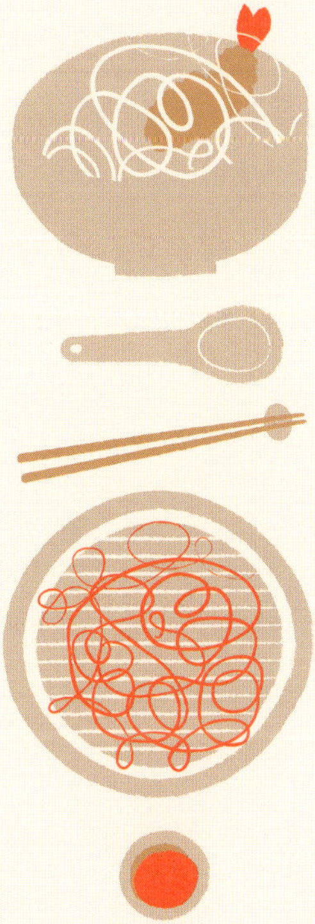

UDON うどん

Udon noodles are made from wheat flour and are dense, chewy, and used in soups and some hot or cold noodle-based salads and stir-fry style dishes. Udon is also perfect when matched with curry or when, like soba in the hotter months, it is served cold with a dipping sauce. We often think that noodle preference is a metaphor for personality. Michelle prefers the delicate, tender and versatile soba noodle and Steve likes the thick, robust and osmotic udon.

EXPECT

- Perfect, chewy noodles, thicker than soba.
- Tasty broth or dipping sauce.

PRICE

- Usually inexpensive to mid-range.

POPULAR WITH ...

- Locals and visitors, students, noodle lovers.

Types

Sanuki (extra thick and chewy, specialty of Kagawa), yaki udon (stir-fried), kitsune (with fried tofu), curry udon, zaru (cold with dipping broth), inaniwa (thick, flat udon).

How to order

Sometimes there will be machines, sometimes not. It's best in hot broth, pairs well with tempura on the side.

Why we love it

Udon is a Tokyo staple. and very versatile like soba; it can be a quick meal or dinner and appears in a range of dishes. Udon is a good counterpoint to the thinner soba noodle if you are in the mood for something more robust.

You must try ...

Both regular and flat udon noodles.

Have with ...

Beer, crispy tempura or fried tofu on the side.

Dine at ...

- Shin Udon, Shinjuku (expect to queue for quite a while).
- Oniyanma, Gotanda.
- Sato Yosuke, Ginza.

UDON YAMACHO

うどん山長

You'll have to queue for this simple yet sophisticated eatery in Ebisu's backstreets. Once inside you'll find warm wooden tables, some two-seaters, some four, and a large communal bench in the middle. Choose from a range of udon soups with extras or a cold udon with dipping broth. You can opt for thin or thick udon, the latter being extra thick, exquisitely chewy and perfect to soak up the flavour of the broth. The tempura here is superb too: lightly crispy and featuring perfectly cooked prawns, vegetables and a cluster of enoki mushrooms. It's Michelle's favourite, while Steve loves the duck with a hint of yuzu. You can also pay a little more for a set meal, which features a main flanked by some memorable side dishes, like the large pieces of bonito (fish) and delicate slices of duck. One of our must visits on every trip.

Ebisu station, east exit

TEMPURA

天ぷら

Tempura is seafood, vegetables, or other ingredients lightly battered and deep-fried. Batter, made from flour, egg, and ice-cold water creates a crisp, airy skin that brings out the flavour of the ingredients. Common tempura fillings are prawns, sweet potatoes, eggplant, mushrooms and shiso leaves. Tempura is served with a delicious dipping sauce called tentsuyu, made of soy sauce, mirin (rice wine) and dashi (stock), and is often accompanied by grated daikon (radish). Amazing on its own, it can also be a superb accompaniment to rice or soba and udon noodles.

EXPECT

- Crispy batter and fresh ingredients.

PRICE

- Usually mid-range to expensive.

POPULAR WITH ...

- Locals and visitors, students, gourmands.

Types

Prawns, vegetable, mountain vegetable, chicken (uncommon), kakiage (mixed vegetable and seafood tempura), tensoba (tempura and soba combined), tempura sushi (tempura in sushi rolls).

How to order

Most tempura eateries will either be al la carte with bowls of rice and side dishes of pickles, or will be part of an udon or soba soup. If a la carte, try to sit up at a bench if there is one and watch the tempura being made in front of you.

Why we love it

Tempura is an absolute staple Japanese meal and pairs well with soups, rice or eaten on its own. A good meal or side dish.

You must try ...

A high-end tempura a la carte meal at some time in your life.

Have with ...

Beer or sake.

Dine at ...

- Tempuraya Miyakawa, Aoyama.
- Kanneko Hannosuke, Nihonbashi.
- Hachimaki, Jimbocho.
- Tempura Nakasei, Asakusa.

TEMPURA TSUNAHACHI

天ぷら つな八

This old-world tempura restaurant in Shinjuku is the flagship store for over 20 tempura specialist eateries across Japan, but it doesn't feel like a chain. It must have seen some changes since it was set up in a meandering two-storey Japanese townhouse in the 1950s (although the original restaurant dates to 1923), but it ignores the encroaching skyscrapers and retail giants and goes about its business of providing excellent tempura to Shinjuku's hungry masses. The service here is fast and friendly and a mid-range price for exceptional, crispy tempura, so expect to queue. Your tempura arrives with a trio of salt, the wasabi salt and black kombu (seaweed) superbly enhance the flavour of tempura and are a real revelation. We recommend grabbing a bench seat and ordering your tempura a la carte to watch the chefs in action. The tiger prawn, pumpkin and aubergine tempura all beg to be ordered, and the set lunch is a seriously good deal.

Shinjuku station, west exit

SUNABA

砂場

Although Sunaba excels at soba noodles, it is also known for its exceptional tempura. Housed in a beautiful building from 1923, Sunaba prides itself on the flavours of the Old Edo period (1603–1867). You can feel the atmosphere of those times, long gone but never forgotten, as you walk into the relaxed interior featuring warm woods, low lamp lights and a black slate floor. Dishes include an Edo-style hot ume (plum) soba which enhances the flavour of the accompanying excellent shrimp and mushroom tempura. The perfectly crispy tempura delicacies can also be a warm up for the main act: a tempura soba that tastes of history, piping broth with two hefty slabs of crispy prawn tempura.

Toranomon station, exit 1

KATSU とんかつ

Katsu are deep-fried cutlets, covered in breadcrumbs, typically made from pork (tonkatsu) or chicken (chicken katsu). Prawns can also get the katsu treatment but they are more often fried as tempura, as are vegetables. Panko breadcrumbs, egg and flour make up the coating, which is then fried creating a crunchy, golden exterior while the inside stays tender. You'll often find katsu served with shredded cabbage, and sometimes on steamed rice as katsudon. The sweet and savoury tonkatsu sauce completes this classic Tokyo comfort food.

EXPECT

- Crispy batter and a tender cutlet inside.
- Very tasty sauce.

PRICE

- Usually cheap to mid-range.

POPULAR WITH ...

- Students, locals and visitors, workers.

Types

Tonkatsu (pork cutlet served with cabbage and sauce), katsudon (pork cutlet with egg and onions over rice), katsu curry (pork cutlet in curry with rice), gyukatsu (beef katsu), ebi katsu (a crispy king prawn, perfect for pescatarians – you can also get fish katsu), kushikatsu (katsu on skewers) menchikatsu (deep fried minced pork, one of Steve's favourite Japanese dishes), vegetable katsu (not that common, but seek it out), katsu sando (pork cutlet sandwich), chicken katsu (chicken version of tonkatsu, often found with rice, sometimes with ramen).

How to order

By menu.

Why we love it

One of the popular classic Japanese dishes. Simple and delicious.

You must try ...

Tonkatsu, katsudon bowl, a katsu curry, a katsu sandwich and a prawn katsu. It's all good.

Have with ...

Sake or beer.

Order extra cabbage. Pour on lashings of sauce.

Dine at ...

- Taiho, Meguro.
- Tonkatsu Marugo, Chiyoda.
- Katsukura, Shinjuku Takashimaya.
- Butagumi, Minato.
- Gyukatsu Motomura, Harajuku.
- Tonkatsu Sugita, Kuramae.

MAISEN

とんかつ まい泉

To say Maisen is a Tokyo institution is an understatement. Slink your way through Harajuku's winding backstreets until you come across this updated traditional bathhouse. Join the queue which can be long but moves quickly and ask to be seated in the beautiful former bathhouse room, with its ornate lattice wood ceiling and low hanging lights, or upstairs in one of the tatami rooms. The pinnacle of the menu is the black pork; smother it in one of Maisen's two signature secret sauces (the thick sweet plum sauce will appear in your dreams), then eat it with mounds of addictive shredded cabbage. If you don't eat pork, the king prawns, sashimi and salads are also excellent. They also do katsu sandwiches from an outside outlet window, the perfect takeout. Several department store food halls have Maisen take-out stands, excellent for shinkansen (bullet train) journeys and picnics.

Omotesando station, exit A2

TONKI

とんかつ とんき

Meat was once banned as a food in Japan, but when this lifted, tonkatsu (crumbed pork) eateries popped up all over Tokyo, forever cementing tonkatsu's status as an indispensable Tokyo fast food. The humble schnitzel was in for a renovation and Tonki, open since 1939 and pretty much unchanged since then, keeps to the old-world recipe: chunky pork in crispy batter with less juice and more character. The roast pork loin has your fat intake covered for the week, memorable, flavourful and dense. Another option, the 'hire,' is leaner. Either way, you'll be queuing before seating yourself on benches placed under low lights around a central 'stage' where you can watch the chefs methodically perform, shaping and grilling their tonkatsu, ready for you to devour. As usual, there are endless refills of that mountainous shredded cabbage plus sides of pickles and miso.

Meguro station, west exit

OTHER FOOD
その他の食べ物

There are so many options to tickle your Tokyo tastebuds. Also try oden (dashi simmered food), eel, obanzai (home-style cooking) and shabu shabu (a specialty hotpot dish). The following is only a snapshot of just some of the delicious options you will have in the city.

TOFU

豆腐

Tofu is a staple part of the Japanese diet and it's versatile and delicious. Firm or silken tofu appears in miso soups, salads, curry and udon (noodle) soup. It's a staple in Chanko Nabe, the hearty, flavoursome soup eaten regularly by sumo wrestlers. Yuba (tofu skin), appears in milky soups or is rolled up and crispy fried. Inari tofu is delicious yuba pockets filled with sweet rice. It's a good source of protein, vitamin B5, calcium, manganese and iron and we love it. Many tofu options are vegetarian however please check stock ingredients to be sure.

GYOZA

餃子

Great with beer, as a side dish or as a starter, gyoza are thin dough dumplings filled with minced pork, cabbage, garlic and ginger. Pan fried for a crispy bottom, then steamed to ensure a tender dumpling, the humble gyoza is hugely popular and can be found dispensed in small eateries and ramen joints. Gyoza come with various dipping sauces, the most popular being made of vinegar and soy sauce. Vegetarian gyoza are rare but becoming increasingly more common (T's Tan Tan do a delicious vegan gyoza, *see* p. 19).

YAKISOBA

焼きそば

Yakisoba is a stir-fried noodle dish made with wheat-based noodles, vegetables, and meat or seafood, often shrimp or pork, which is seasoned with a savoury-sweet sauce. Usually cooked on a griddle, yakisoba is a staple at festival or temple street stalls but can also be found in casual eateries. It's most often garnished with aonori (seaweed powder), pickled ginger and mayonnaise.

SUKIYAKI

すき焼き

Sukiyaki is a hot-pot dish with thinly sliced beef, tofu, vegetables and noodles in a sweet-savoury broth of soy sauce, sugar and mirin (rice wine). Sukiyaki is often cooked at the table in a shallow iron pan and enjoyed by dipping ingredients into raw egg. Perfect for gatherings and celebrations, it's a classic one-pot meal that is often served with rice and garland chrysanthemum.

OKONOMIYAKI

お好み焼き

One of the simplest and best meals in Japan, okonomiyaki is essentially a glorified omelette, but the added cabbage, spring onions, bonito flakes, pork, seafood, and/or cheese and the toppings of mayonnaise and rich okonomiyaki sauce take it to the next level. You'll often get the ingredients and 'compile' your own okonomiyaki at a table with a grill, but there are also eateries where experts make them for you. It's best known in Hiroshima and Osaka, but Tokyo has a flair for okonomiyaki as well.

DONBURI

丼もの

Steve is a fan of this bowl of steamed rice topped with a variety of ingredients, such as meat, fish, vegetables or eggs. It's a simple dish, cheap and fast. Try gyudon (beef), oyakodon (chicken and egg), and katsudon (pork cutlet). Comfort food alert!

YAKITORI

焼き鳥

The perfect fast food and street food, yakitori is simply cuts of chicken on skewers grilled over an open flame. Yakitori can be enjoyed at street stalls, izakaya (pubs with small plate food) and even from food halls and konbini (convenience stores). It is perfect with booze. Yakitori cuts can vary and include chicken meatballs (tsukune), thigh (momo), thigh with spring onion (negima) and chicken skin (kawa). Other options like cartilage or 'hormone' can be tried by the culinary adventurer.

CURRY

カレー

Japanese curry serves a similar function to Indian curry and yet has quite a different flavour profile. Excellent with rice, it is versatile and can completely change a dish of udon (noodle), tonkatsu (crumbed pork) or even soup. A popular Japanese comfort food, it is rich, savoury, slightly sweet and notably less spicy than an Indian curry. It will often feature onions, carrots and potatoes, and chicken or beef, but there are vegetarian options (try **Curry House CoCo Ichibanya**).

KONBINI
コンビニ

Konbini (Japanese convenience stores) are ubiquitous across the nation's capital, and it's fair to say they will save your life at some point with a computer chord or phone charger, power up drink (Pocari Sweat, extreme green tea), woolly socks, mittens in winter and cooling products in summer. Aisles of unexpected items jump out at you, and the packaging and product design alone is enough to make you spend hours in one of these amazing places. ATMs and ticket sales, scanners and printers, it's all in the one place, truly a convenience store. Unlike in many other countries, food is of a good standard with sweets, drinks, booze and fast food (onigiri rice balls, noodles and salads, etc) at excellent prices. We buy a konbini meal for a park picnic or room picnic or for a longer train journey to accompany our ekiben (train bento). Lawson, 7-Eleven NewDays (run by JR East) and FamilyMart all vie for your attention with their home-brand products. Lawson's genius marketing has rolled out a side brand 'Natural' which proudly sells brown rice onigiri and all manner of healthier snacks and more thoughtful eco packaging.

Over the years we have gathered our own collection of favourite food purchases for all meals of the day. We share them with you here:

BREAKFAST

Steve & Michelle: R1 yoghurt, dorayaki (red bean pancake), fruit, cold Boss coffee.

SNACKS

Steve & Michelle: Kameda soft salad rice crackers, kameda kakinotane (rice crackers and peanut snack), fresh edamame.

LUNCH & DINNER

Steve: Tuna, salmon or chicken onigiri (rice balls), chicken bento, potato salad, tuna and tamago sando (one half egg sandwich, one half tuna sandwich), sneaky fried chicken from the counter at Lawson.

Michelle: Natural Lawson onigiri (rice balls) with edamame or pickles, seaweed salad, tamago sando (egg sandwich), Pino (small ice-cream bites), frozen mochi.

DINNER

Steve: Onigiri (rice balls), various meat bento, potato salad, tempura cake pot noodles, purin (custard pudding), Country Ma'am treats, Pino (small ice-cream bites), white chocolate covered strawberries, Crunky chocolate bar.

Michelle: Veggie onigiri (rice balls), seaweed salad, edamame, miso pot soup, Ts Vegan Noodles (Natural Lawson), annin tofu (sweet milk jelly), Lotte Yukimi Daifuku (mochi ice-cream), Bouncing Punipuni Mochi ice-cream, Meiji milk chocolate.

BOOZE

Steve: Strong Zero, highball (whisky soda).

Michelle: Choya One Cup Plum Wine, Calpis sour, lemon sour.

EXTRAS

Steve: Liver shot for after a seedy night.

Michelle: Collagen shot or Vitamin C shot for a heathy holiday glow.

OMIYAGE

Don't forget to buy treats that can act as omiyage (regional souvenirs). This is your opportunity to be adventurous and fill your bag with inexpensive presents to blow the minds of your most adventurous culinary friends.

CULTURE NOTE

If you want to deep dive into convenience store culture in preparation for your trip, Sayaka Murata's novel *Convenience Store Woman* embodies the tone and flavour of these ubiquitous chains dotted on almost every corner of Tokyo.

TSUKIJI OUTER MARKET
築地場外市場

Tsukiji

4 Tsukiji, Chuo-ku
Mon–Tues & Thurs–Sat 10am–8pm, Wed 10am–3pm
‣ Tsukiji station, exit 2
tsukiji.or.jp

With fish caught that morning found in a plethora of reasonably priced sushi eateries like **Itadori Bekkan** (*see* p. 79), you could say the outer market is a must-do destination for anyone, but especially for the seafood aficionado. There are an abundance of sushi and sashimi eateries, most of which are relatively cheap compared to many Tokyo sushi restaurants. They are often open from very early in the morning and queues can form for hours in the most popular ones. Tiny eateries and takeaway joints can be found on the outer rim of the market, inside the market and down discreet wafer-thin alleys. Most sushi is of excellent standard, delicate, melt-in-your-mouth and decidedly memorable. The atmosphere is casual, with simple seating arrangements in street stalls where you crouch low on crates or at a side stand open to the alleys. The variety of takeaway fresh produce is remarkable. Crab claws and legs piled high, giant oysters from Kumamoto and Hokkaido, sweet omelette squares, buns stuffed with uni (sea urchin) and the market's signature fatty tuna are all prepped and packaged to perfection. Adventurous foodies will not be disappointed by the seasonality, range and presentation.

CRABS PARADISE 築地
大集合
築地 かに祭
red king ¥3,000
red king ¥2,000
Please use the seats ↑ on the second floor↑
蟹料理

鮪 TUNA
本日の日替り
海鮮丼
魚介9種入り
Special Selected Kaisendon
9 kinds of seafoods

SHOKUPAN
食パン

Pelican
BRAND

Western food gained popularity in Japan after World War II and yoshoku (Japanese spins on Western-style dishes) can be one of the most delicious and interesting experiences while in Tokyo. Shokupan is a very high tin loaf in comparison to Western bread standards, a little bit sweet, and very soft and fluffy. This style of Japanese milk bread has become popular all over the world and is a must try. 'Big toast' is one of our favourite breakfast staples with kissaten (vintage coffee house) serving up butter toast, honey toast, pizza toast, cheese toast and tamago (egg) and fruit sandos. The fluffiest white bread with a spongy pull-apart quality, the art of milk bread is expressed through size, symmetry, taste and packaging. There is intense speculation on the density and usage of the bread for each day of its life, best for sandwiches on day one and for toast on day three, etc. Bread is a popular gift in Tokyo which explains why bakery branding is impressive and bread products are packaged to perfection.

For a premium quality loaf (with a serious price to match) **Ginza Nishikawa** (Ginza-Itchome station, exit 10) has decadent built-in ingredients like cream butter and honey, making it delicious on its own. Ginza's **Centre the Bakery** (Ginza-Itchome station, exit 3) is a bakery/ cafe where you can select shokupan and pair it with delicious jams and different types of butter. You can also choose a toaster that appeals to your personality, and toast your shokupan at the table. Since 1942, Tawaramachi's **Pelican Bakery** (Tawaramachi station, exit 3) has honed its art, perfecting a white loaf and fluffy dinner rolls — the only items for sale. The adorable pinky-red hooded canopy and vintage logo invite you into a delicious smelling store. This Tokyo institution is popular and will require you to queue. When the bread is sold out, they will pack up for the day so arrive early. Owned by the same family for four generations, much of the bread is reserved on an ordering system so you may need to ask your hotel to secure your reservation. Nearby **Pelican Café** (Tawaramachi station, exit 2) has a delicious array of toast and sandwiches all made with its signature bread.

LITTLE NAP COFFEE STAND
リトルナップコーヒースタンド

Yoyogi

5-65-4 Yoyogi, Shibuya-ku

Tues–Sun 9am–7pm

‣ Yoyogi-Hachiman station, exit 3

littlenap.jp

We like to park our bicycles out the front of Little Nap and head into the coffee pit stop opposite sprawling Yoyogi park, well and truly ready for a morning coffee. Not so much a cafe as a stylish shoebox, Little Nap was one of Yoyogi's early coffee adopters and the retro American-style signage, big maps on the walls and bags of rustic charm (literally, as bags of coffee beans are strewn about the place) set the scene for one of Tokyo's cosier contemporary coffee houses. Seating is limited to a few stools inside and a long bench outside, which we like to settle onto with our coffees as we watch morning Yoyogi go about its business. The excellent drip coffee, along with the perfectly made expresso, has earned the miniscule, plucky coffee stand its name as the go-to place for anyone finding themselves in need of a pick-me-up mid-morning or after a picnic and a 'little nap' in Yoyogi park.

SWITCH COFFEE
スイッチコーヒー

Meguro

1-17-23 Meguro, Meguro-ku

Mon–Sun 10am–7pm

‣ Meguro station, west exit

switchcoffeetokyo.com

We recently meandered off the main drag of Meguro-dori to revisit this hole-in-the-wall coffee stand which had impressed us when it was a fledgling coffee store in 2015. We had written it into one of our first books, *Tokyo Precincts*, having stumbled across it after eating at a much-hyped eatery called Beard (since sadly closed down). Everything about Switch is done well; the exterior is stylish and the row of glass coffee pots along the counter is a deft touch. This is a takeaway kind of joint with no seats, but you can rest on a small wooden bench outside. Staff here are friendly and knowledgeable; they talk about coffee like it is fine wine, referring to regions, bean varieties and fruit aromas. They might suggest that a blend has a hint of blueberry jam or an afterglow of sweet brown sugar. If a particular blend takes your fancy, you can buy beans in 250gm packets to go. Terms like 'single origin' and 'Costa Rican dragon' can make you feel like you are getting your hands on something illicit, and the coffee is so good you may as well be.

TRAVELLER'S NOTE

Be sure to visit Switch's other store just opposite Yoyogi-Hachiman station and their more expansive **Switch Coffee K**, housed in an impressive 1920s' bank building.

PICNICS
ピクニック

A wonderful option for meals in the summer and the warmer months in Tokyo is a picnic in one of Tokyo's beautiful green spaces. It's such a fun way to experience a variety of food options with a group, family or even a romantic alfresco lunch just for two. We love to hire bikes, cycle to our favourite green space laden with goodies and while away the afternoon. Our day from 11am will go something like the Ebisu itinerary on this page, however you have all the resources to make your own versions.

FAVOURITE PICNIC SPACES NOTE

We recommend **Rinshinomori park**, **Imperial Palace** outer garden, **Kinuta park**, **Showa Memorial park**, the rooftop at **Isetan** in Shinjuku, and **Yoyogi park**. Romantics might like to ride the swan boats that can be found paddling around the lakes in **Inokashira park** and **Ueno park** (*see* p. 67).

Start at Ebisu station (or your own location)

1. Buy a hot or cold green tea (or make one in the hotel) and decant into a travel drink bottle.
2. Hire a bike (hellocycling.jp).
3. Scope out **Atre** in Ebisu station for delicious food options.
4. Stop at **Onigiri Ishin Ebisu Ten** near the east exit of Ebisu station for delicious and very portable rice triangles.
5. Cycle to our favourite hole-in-the-wall shop **Taiyaki Hiiragi** (fish-shaped pastry filled with bean paste).
6. Hit a konbini (convenience store) for a vast choice of snacks.

BEASTY COFFEE (CAFÉ LABORATORY)

ビースティー コーヒー カフェ ラボラトリー

Tomigaya

1-19-3 Tomigaya, Shibuya-ku

Mon–Sun 8am–8pm

‣ Yoyogi-Koen station, exit 4

beastycoffee.com

This hole-in-the-wall-meets-tiny-cafe spills onto the breezy streets of Tomigaya, a welcome refuel as you sift through the laid-back vintage and local clothing stores. We find that Beasty Coffee is one of the best, with robust roasts and a range of coffee options that should please the coffee snob and the casual sipper alike. You can sit inside, the minimal concrete and wood interior is industrial chic, but if the outside bench is free, grab it and do a spot of people watching while you sip on Beasty's cold brew, lattes or their excellent mocha. Their powerful long black should shake even the sleepiest of heads awake. There are also some tasty nibbles and they even brew their own craft beer – the vats can be seen in a small room at the back of the store.

KOFFEE MAMEYA KAKERU
コーヒー マメヤ カケル

Kiyosumi

2-16-14 Hirano, Koto-ku

Mon–Sun 11am–6pm

‣ Kiyosumi-Shirakawa station, exit A3

koffee-mameya.com

The Kiyosumi area has been on our map for a while. It's home to **MOT**, the Museum of Contemporary Art (*see* p. 69), and one of Tokyo's best landscaped stroll gardens, the unsung **Kiyosumi Teien garden** (*see* p. 197), as well as **Heart Street** with its small bookstores and vintage stores. The area has also become known as 'coffee town.' Omotesando stalwart Mameya Koffee's new cafe in Kiyosumi, Koffee Mameya Kakeru, is perfectly placed between the gallery and the garden. Eiichi Kunitomo's superb coffee is still sold from what looks like a science lab in a large wooden box, only now you can't buy a coffee to go, you have to book for an intense coffee tasting experience. Places are booked out in advance so you'll need to book before you head to Japan. Mameya translates as 'bean shop' and a wall of beans appears before you, giving you the perfect opportunity to take some of Mameya's barista choice coffee bean blends home to make that perfect brew.

KABUKI
蕪木

Kuramae

1-12-12 Misuji, Taito-ku

Mon–Fri 10am–5pm
Sat–Sun 9am–8pm

‣ Kuramae station, exit A3

Kabuki exists in a small, elegant space where it elevates coffee to high art and performance, just like its namesake. You could easily walk past the chic yet secretive door on the fringes of the Kuramae neighbourhood. A small sign declares in kanji that you have arrived at Kabuki, a contemporary kissaten (vintage coffee house) which specialises in pairing two types of bean, coffee and chocolate. They roast beans on-site and sell fresh beans to coffee connoisseurs, but the casual caffeine addict can enter the beautiful space for a coffee experience that pairs slow, hand drip, expertly made coffee with a wafer-thin slice of exquisite dark chocolate. The interior matches the experience, with warm, chunky woods and antique dark-wood cabinets and benches where elegant, vintage-style china and highly polished cutlery add further other-wordly elegance to the proceedings. It's a quiet place, not for casual chat; a place to savour coffee, the aroma, the flavour and the ambience, while a soundtrack of soft jazz floats in the air.

AREA NOTE

Make sure you also visit local favourites **Allpress Coffee**, **Arise Coffee Roasters**, **Blue Bottle Coffee**, **Sunday Zoo Coffee** and **Fukadaso Cafe**.

NARA KIKUSUIRO UNAKIKU
奈良菊水楼 うな菊

Sekiguchi

2-10-8 Sekiguchi, Bunkyo-ku

Mon–Sun 11am–3pm & 5–9pm

‣ Edogawabashi station, exit 1A

kikusuiro.com/unakiku

First opened in 1891 in Japan's original capital Nara, the very epicentre of culture, this chic eel restaurant now has a branch in the lush gardens of luxury Hotel Chinzanso. Opened in 2016 and refurbished in 2023, this branch of the famed restaurant has a variety of set meals which highlight eel. A stroll through the verdant garden, with its pagoda, bridges and bamboo groves, will immediately take you out of the mindset of the concrete jungle. The characterful hut hidden amongst the groves will confirm your suspicion that you have stepped through a portal and entered another time. The dishes are prepared in the traditional manner using Edomae-unagi eel. Kikusuiro also prides itself on the sauce, the result of many years of perfection, which is unique to this eel restaurant. Whether you want to go for a moderately priced set lunch or dinner or you're keen on the memorable unagi kaiseki feast, Kikusuiro will be an experience that you will be talking about for years to come.

HIGASHI-YAMA
ヒガシヤマ

Meguro

1-21-25 Higashiyama, Meguro-ku

Mon–Fri 6–10pm

‣ Nakameguro station, west exit

higashiyama-tokyo.jp

Washoku is essentially traditional Japanese food and if you want to see it elevated to an art form, Higashi-Yama is the place to go. Design company Simplicity has put its know-how into both the space and the food. The exquisite décor, the delicious fare, the flowing regional sake and the 'I-need-that-in-my-house-right-now' ceramics and utensils make this a memorable dining experience. The artfully arranged, jewel-like segmented boxes highlighting seasonal Japanese dishes are accompanied by plates with delicately arranged, perfectly flavoured dishes that will instantly make it onto your 'best of' list. The dining space is beautiful at night when the warm woods of the tables and counter seating are turned into an intimate experience by the subtle lighting. Fashion conscious locals referred to as tarento (the talent), are regular customers, eager to return for the tender wagyu beef cutlet, melt-in-the-mouth squid, zara-dofu (soybean tofu), sashimi (sliced expertly in front of you) and seasonal vegetables like white asparagus, all of which, when we dined there, were memorably rounded off by a green tea panna cotta for dessert.

AREA NOTE

Afterwards, why not head into the Chinzanso hotel bar Le Marquis for one of their signature cocktails, the Camellia Martini?

Much of Asakusa has kept its old-world Edo period (1603–1867) charm, and you can get involved by eating at long-standing noodle houses, tempura specialists and yakitori joints that adhere to classic Edo recipes. Head to **Namiki Yabu Soba** for authentic 'worker' soba noodle soups at yesterday's prices. For ramen, visit **Bazoku** where the handmade noodles have been rated for decades, their spicy tantanmen (ramen) reveals both the art of the original Chinese dish and the Japanese influence. If you are after the finest tempura, join the locals at **Sansada** which has been around for about 160 years! Fans of deep fried, battered pork should line up at **Katsukichi**, which has 50 different styles of tonkatsu. If you want to try the Tokyo specialty of unagi (eel), then don't miss **Hatsuogawa**, Tokyo's oldest eel restaurant, which earned itself a Michelin Bib Gourmand. For onigiri, head to **Yadoroku**, Tokyo's oldest onigiri joint (are you seeing a theme here?), which has perfected the popular rice triangle snack over its nearly 70 years in operation and has a Bib Gourmand too. Don't miss **Sugita Tonkatsu** in Kuramae, run by second-generation chef Mitsuo Sato, who prides himself on excellent ingredients and a 'two-pot' system that delivers tonkatsu that is both tender on the inside and and perfectly crispy outside. If you have a sweet tooth, head into **Nishiyama**, serving wagashi (Japanese sweets) since the 1850s. In fact, long-standing, family owned wagashi stores are a spiritual crusade in Asakusa. Try **Usagiya** for perfect dorayaki pancakes (since 1914) and **Kamejuu**.

AREA NOTE

Nakamise-dori, on the way up to Senso-ji, has many old-style street stalls with a memorable array of classic snacks that visitors to the temple during the Edo period would have eaten.

HAGISO
はぎそう

Yanaka

3-10-25 Yanaka, Taito-ku
Mon–Sun 11am–11pm
‣ Sendagi station, exit 1
hagiso.com/hagiso

Although Hagiso still shows off its centuries-old rustic charm and the wooden beams and pillars recall the old house the cafe is set up in, this is new Yanaka at its finest. The cafe has been updated with clean, minimalist lines and the food is modern, with only the slightest nod to traditional Japanese fare. Laze away the afternoon on your laptop, sipping brew coffee and munching on cake with the locals, or stroll through the contemporary gallery, a gleaming sliver just to the side of the cafe, to get up-to-date with challenging new contemporary art. Lunch sets are good value, and the keema curry, with a fried egg plonked on top, goes down well with one of Hagiso's craft beers. The perfect Yanaka backstreet refuel.

CHUM APARTMENT
チャム アパートメント

Meguro

4-12-17 Megurohoncho, Meguro-ku

Tues–Wed 11.30am–5.30pm, Thurs–Sun 11.30am–10pm

‣ Musashi-Koyama station, west exit

chum-apt.net

Japanese artist Chiharu Yoshikawa took a run-down mansion in a quiet Meguro backstreet and turned it into local hotspot Chum (pronounced 'charm') Apartment. The relaxed space looks like a Spanish villa in the '70s and the simple Italian-inspired menu adds to the laid-back feeling. A Moroccan colour palette hues the peeling, dishevelled walls and iron lattice work doors, crosses, skulls and low-lit chandeliers lend the space a hint of oddball chic. It's cosy, with deep couches and repurposed furniture that add a 'drop in' element to the overall cafe-cum-bar-cum-shop. Settle in for a daily set lunch, which includes coffee or tea. Chum is open late as it nears the weekend, so come back at night, slip into one of the many nooks and crannies in the cafe, which by now has morphed into a bar, and order a wine, craft beer or shochu (distilled spirit). We guarantee you'll feel like a local.

NIHONBASHI YUKARI
日本橋ゆかり

Nihonbashi

3-2-14 Nihonbashi, Chuo-ku

Mon–Sat 11am–2pm, 5–10pm

‣ Tokyo Station, Yaesu exit

nihonbashi-yukari.com

Owned and run by Kimio Nonaga, former 'Iron Chef' champion, Nihonbashi Yukari offers immaculate cuisine at better-than-expected prices. The chic interior adds to the impression that you are about to drop some yen, but the seasonal deluxe bento lunch sets are surprisingly well priced (make sure that you order in advance when you make your reservation). Our lunch box included melt-in-the-mouth sashimi and tofu, tasting plates of grilled meats and other elegant dishes, artfully arranged with delicate flower garnishes. Each small, exquisite course of this bento banquet will make you feel like you're dining with the emperor, or at least Chairman Kaga (aka Shigekatsu Katsuta, host of 'Iron Chef'). If memory serves me correctly, 'Iron Chef' was very popular. This is a meal you'll never forget at a price you'll barely notice. Bookings are essential.

MEALS ARE DELIGHTFUL
ミールズ アー
デライトフル

Tomigaya

1-17-5 Tomigaya, Shibuya-ku

Thurs–Tues 11.30am–5.30pm

› Yoyogi-Hachiman station, exit 4.

marumitsu.jp/m_a_d

This gentle haven, run by Marumitsu Poterie in a quiet backstreet of Tomigaya, has a simple menu featuring two set meals of the day, or, as they say, 'one soup, and three'. The teishoku (meal sets) styled simple fare is delicious and consists of, as the name suggests, a soup and three accompaniments. On the day we were there, we had a flavoured rice and some immaculate stewed pork with a hearty miso soup and an enhanced salad. Meals will be followed by a small sweet, perhaps a homemade ice-cream. Sitting in the updated Taisho period (1912–26) building, you feel like you are in someone's living room eating with friends and family. The kitchen running lengthwise along the room says otherwise – this place is serious about elevating simple food and it does it superbly. Of course, this means that there is always a queue, especially on weekends, but less so on weekdays, so time your visit right. You can also book on weekdays if you know the exact time of your arrival and are happy to do a sitting in a two-hour timeframe.

DESIGN NOTE

The back of the Meals Are Delightful store features a tastefully curated selection of **Marumitsu Poterie** ceramics and quality homewares that reflect the early 20th-century style of the 2nd-floor room.

OHITSUZENTANBO YOYOGI MAIN STORE
おひつ膳 田んぼ
代々木本店

Yoyogi

1-41-9 Yoyogi, Shibuya-ku

Mon–Sun 8am–8.30pm

‣ Yoyogi station, exit A1

tanbo.co.jp

Ohitsu makes teishoku set meals (ohitsuzen) that highlight their superior quality rice, which is served in ohitsu (small wooden buckets) with a side kettle of green tea for pouring over the rice in the traditional way. The meals come with a main – the choice is extensive and everything is superb. Black cod, skipjack tuna, pork, sashimi, you can't go wrong. Added to this is wasabi, herb miso and small 'rice bubbles' which are a fabulous textural addition to the meal. Extras can be ordered – the tamagoyaki (omelette) and onigiri (rice balls) are superb, so is the miso, included with your set. Open all day, conveniently for breakfast, lunch or early dinner, there is always a queue. Just how long that queue is will depend on what time you go, so if you can time your hunger to come at an 'off peak' time, you'll spend less time dreaming of your meal in the line, and more time sitting down at the wooden tables in the cute traditional interior, enjoying your rustic-tinged feast.

GOHANYA ISSHIN
ごはんや 一芯

Daikanyama

1-30-3 Sarugakucho, Shibuya-ku

Mon–Sun 11.30am–2pm, 5–11pm

‣ Daikanyama station, north exit

g775402.gorp.jp

Chances are the queue will have already formed and will be snaking around the side street even before Isshin has opened for lunch, but it has earned such a reputation with locals, especially on a weekend or holiday, that you will almost always have to wait for an hour at least. It's worth it though – the cosy warm wood, comfy seating and contemporary chic allure of the interior are just an amuse-bouche, and the menu is the star. It's complex in its simplicity, set meals that highlight rice (ohitsumeshi – rice cooked in a triple baked earthenware donabe pot) and add a main accompaniment, tempura, perfectly cooked tamagoyaki (omelette) and superbly flavoursome crispy karaage (fried chicken). Miso and pickles complete the mini feast. It's a kind of upscaling of the simple teishoku (meal sets) and pairs wonderfully with an expertly chosen selection of sake. The lunch sets are a steal by today's prices as well, and definitely part of the reason why long lines form before opening time. To avoid the lines, go at night for the a la carte selection, but the price point is somewhat higher.

DOUGHNUTS
ドーナツ

In Tokyo, the doughnut is as ubiquitous as coffee or tea, and they come in a wide variety of stores from hole-in-the-wall takeaway joints to sit-down cafes. All will have a particular spin, whether it be the ingredients, which can range from soy-pulp and tofu to specially fermented yeasts, to super-cute doughnuts in the shape of characters or animals. American doughnut franchises are big, even if they no longer exist anywhere else in the world. Murakami's characters (and possibly Murakami) were fond of **Dunkin' Donuts**, and **Mister Donut** make the super cute Pon de Lion, a lion head-shaped doughnut, that is everywhere.

It's the smaller, contemporary makers however, who are really making a scene. Case in point is the popularity of **I'm Donut?** (*see* p. 113), Kobe's **Hara Donuts**, with stores in Meguro (Meguro station, west exit), and Kichijoji (Kichijoji station, west exit) make petite circular treats from tofu pulp. Less sweet and healthier (well slightly), Hara's delicious flavours include white chocolate and matcha, but there are over 80 taste sensations, so visit often. **Floresta Nature Doughnuts** (Koenji station, north exit) describe themselves as 'guilt free'. They're organic and handmade instore. The major drawcard here though is the cute animal shapes that the doughnuts come in, including cats, rabbits, frogs and tigers. The ears are usually crunchy, a nice touch. Behind the sliding door of Yoyogi-Uehara's **Haritts** (Yoyogi-uehara staion, east exit), you'll find the handmade doughnut has been perfected, a perfectly soft, perfectly chewy treat with popular flavours including cinnamon raisin or cream cheese, both of which have a habit of running out early. Also visit **Good Town Donuts**, **Hocus Pocus** and **Dumbo Donuts and Coffee**.

I'M DONUT?
アイム ドーナツ

Nakameguro

1-22-10 Kamimeguro, Meguro-ku

Mon–Sun 9am–7pm

‣ Nakameguro station, east exit

A doughnut is a 'dough' nut, right? Not in Japan, where doughnuts can be made from ingredients as diverse as soy pulp or mochi. In the case of I'm Donut? the delectable treats are 'nama style', a process where yeast-leavened dough makes them an irresistible amalgam of extra fluffy yet slightly chewy. The question mark says it all, is it a doughnut? Or something more? Nakameguro's hole-in-the-wall outlet was the original store and is a magnet for locals and tourists. It's a photograph waiting to be taken sure, but mostly it's a delectable treat worth lining up for and people do just that, mouths drooling at the thought of the upcoming delight. As with any queue, choose your time to reduce the duration of your impatient wait. However, it's an agony of choice as you have to also bear in mind that flavours can run out and with a list including custard, framboise, pistachio and, erm, prosciutto, you might want to get there early, or secretively uncover a time when batches arrive.

TORAYA AKASAKA FLAGSHIP STORE
虎屋菓寮 赤坂店

Akasaka

4-9-22 Akasaka, Minato-ku

Mon–Sun 8.30am–7pm

‣ Akasaka-mitsuke station, exit A

toraya-group.co.jp/shops/shop-5

With an over 500-year history, Toraya is one of Japan's premium wagashi (traditional Japanese confection) makers. A Kyoto business, Toraya set up its first Tokyo store in 1879. The flagship Tokyo store was built in 1964, but little trace of the old building remains. History has had a complete rewrite in this towering glass semicircle that looks out over Aoyama-dori, an extensive renovation that had its official opening in 2018. Glass might be the theme outside, but inside it's all about the wood, which plays out in booths, staircases and a spectacular vaulted ceiling. On the 3rd floor you can relax with a quality coffee or tea, but it's the sweets you came for. Choose from a teetering kakigori (shaved ice dessert), anmitsu (adzuki bean and agar jelly in syrup), oshiruko (sweet red bean soup) or a selection of wagashi including Toraya's famous yokan (jellied bean paste), which comes in colourful layers or as a block wrapped in bamboo leaves. We developed a taste for yokan many years ago on our first trip to Japan, and never miss an opportunity to visit Toraya to pick up a delicate, artistically shaped sweet to savour with a park picnic.

CULTURE NOTE

Toraya hosts a small museum and gallery with some impressive sweet-making tools from days gone by.

DACO BREAD MUSEUM
ダコー

Nakameguro

1-3-18 Kamimeguro, Meguro-ku

Mon–Sun 11am–8pm

‣ Nakameguro station, east exit

The side hussle of **I'm Donut?** (*see* p. 113), Daco Bread is self-described as a 'bread museum'. You won't find fossilised loaves here however, but fresh bread, sandwiches, rolls and tasty pastries which can be enjoyed in the colourful and quirky contemporary interior or outside where you can watch the relaxed Nakameguro crowd strolling around the streets. The architecturally designed room is an organic, freeform space age pod – if you don't like having your photo taken you may find it hard to dodge the influencers and snap happy holidaymakers. Snuggle up in a booth and enjoy your omelette rustique or briossant (as it sounds, a brioche croissant hybrid) or fruit sand (a bun that emulates the popular fruit sando) with a blood orange matcha or fruit hojicha latte, just a couple of the 50+ drinks on offer. The shaved ice kakigori is highly recommended in summer. As an added bonus, if you can't be bothered queuing for an hour up the road, you can find a small curation of I'm Donut? treats in-store.

DANDELION CHOCOLATE, FACTORY & CAFE
ダンデライオン・チョコレート ファクトリー&カフェ

Kuramae

4-14-6 Kuramae, Taito-ku

Mon–Sun 10am–7pm

‣ Kuramae station, exit A0 or A3

dandelionchocolate.jp

A light, airy and open architecturally designed space in Kuramae sets up the perfect destination for anyone with a sweet tooth. If you want artisan-crafted chocolate, Dandelion is your Willy Wonka factory in the heart of this relaxed area. Self-described by San Francisco entrepreneur owners as 'bean to bar', the craft chocolate aesthetic is in front of you when you arrive, with rooms stacked high with bags of cocoa beans, about to meet their fate in large stainless-steel vats and machines. The abundant staff move about in a constant state of activity over large workbenches which are spread out under an impressive, vaulted ceiling. The Chef's Tasting Set gives you a chance to see the dessert skills on display, both a visual and culinary treat featuring a lemon tart, crème brûlée, financier, profiterole and gelee de cacao fruits. Head upstairs to relax with your choice, and don't forget to pair it with a delicious hot or cold chocolate drink and, dare we say, add the chocolate brownie set? It helps to have company here so you can try everything and convince yourself that you didn't order too much. Your chocolate coma should keep you going for the rest of the day.

Amazon cacao fruits
210yen (226)
Kouign amann
sweet potato
350yen (378)

BRASIL
TANZANIA
BELIZE
GUATEMALA
HONDURAS

TORAYA AN STAND
トラヤあんスタンド

Aoyama

3-12-16 Kita Aoyama, Minato-ku

Mon–Sun 11am–7pm

‣ Omotesando station, exit B2

anstand.toraya-group.co.jp

Toraya is one of Japan's oldest and most revered makers of 'an wagashi', a traditional sweet made from adzuki red bean paste. For over 500 years their exquisite shapes, designs and packaging have been the pinnacle of beauty and held up as the country's finest, showcased in their spectacular Akasaka flagship store (*see* p. 114). The much more petite An Stand in Aoyama still features red bean paste as a key ingredient, but it is updated to blend with a mix of Western-style drinks and desserts as well as Japanese favourites. Try the unique red bean paste latte, a coffee with bean paste stirred into it. Other surprises include red bean paste on toast, in a giant cookie and a bread style éclair where the bean paste complements a cream cheese filling. The store is a minimal, architectural two-storey treasure. Sip your bean coffee while posing on the stone sculpture outside, or share your sweets upstairs with the cute tiger (Toraya's namesake mascot) prowling in the corner.

SHIROIKURO
しろいくろ

Azabu-Juban

2-8-1 Azabu-Juban, Minato-ku

Mon–Sun 10am–6pm

‣ Azabu-Juban station, exit 1

shiroikuro.com

Strolling the fascinating Azabu-Juban backstreets will eventually bring you to this tiny, chic dessert store. Mochi, ice-cream and cake are on the menu, and although the Japanese palate for sweets is delicate, anyone with a craving for sugar will find themselves pleasantly surprised and satisfied. A white cat on noren curtains will usher you into a modern rework of an old Japanese house. Meaning 'Black and White', Shiroikuro's name is fitting as many of its delicious delicacies have a sweet white exterior that hides a dense black soybean centre. Enjoy them by dining in, or take them away for a delectable picnic dessert. The most eye-catching sweet is probably the 'Swiss Roll', or salted black bean roll cake (available in black or white), a scrumptious yet unfamiliar version of the classic European cake, but the popular choice is the black bean salt daifuku (stuffed mochi) perfectly accompanied by the black bean tea. In summer, treat yourself to a cooling, delicious salted black bean ice-cream. If you happen to be at Shiroikuro in autumn, that's when the new black beans arrive, so try the freshest possible treats available.

AREA NOTE

NEWoMan (Shinjuku station, south exit) is also home to a Toraya An Stand.

SEASONAL NOTE

In summer, treat yourself to a cooling, delicious salted black bean ice-cream. If you happen to be at Shiroikuro in autumn, that's when the new black beans arrive, so try the freshest possible treats available.

WESTERN-INFLUENCED SWEETS
洋風スイーツ

It's no secret that Tokyo has a love affair with Paris, much of which reveals itself in an obsession with the French patisserie. As a result, some of the world's finest sweet treats can be found in Tokyo, rivalling anything you may find in Europe. Perennial favourites such as macarons, éclairs, baumkuchen (layered cake) or roll cake are infused with Japanese ingredients such as green tea or yuzu while a distinctly Japanese spin is given to a crepe cake, parfait and cheesecake. Sweet treats are displayed like petite works of art on counters and in cabinets throughout Tokyo. Wandering around a departo's food hall sets the scene for what you can expect from a sit down, eat in, dessert experience. Expect exquisite service, an array of mouth-watering choices and crockery and cutlery to complete the artistic aesthetic. When choosing a dessert, we always select a seasonal delicacy, for example chestnuts in autumn or strawberries in spring. East-meets-west flavours and superb presentation make an afternoon tea (or an any time of the day treat) a distinctly memorable Tokyo experience.

Some unmissable Tokyo patisserie include: **Patisserie Kyohei Mikami** (Yoga station, east exit), **Pierre Hermé Paris Aoyama** (Omotesando station, exit B2) and the delightfully retro **Shiseido Parlour Salon de Café** (Ginza station, exit A2).

PATISSERIE SADAHARU AOKI PARIS
パティスリー・サダハル・アオキ・パリ東京ミッドタウン店
Roppongi

Aoki is well known in Paris for his patisserie that gives classic French cakes and sweets a surprising Japanese twist. It seems fitting to eat his creations in Tokyo, where he first started developing his ideas at the city's Machida Cooking School. You'll likely find Steve on each of our trips peering through the window of the store in Tokyo Midtown in the hope of spying the Aoki holy grail, the matcha éclair, with its green icing showing a spin on the classic French cake, a hint of matcha bringing a slight bitterness to the flavour profile, echoed in the matcha cream inside. There are other Japanese/French treats as well. We recommend the matcha or the yuzu macaron and, if you're game, why not opt for the wasabi macaron? Sadaharu Aoki stores can also be found in Shinjuku's Isetan and Marunouchi.

Tokyo Midtown Galleria B1F, 9-7-4 Akasaka, Roppongi, Minato-ku

Mon–Sun 11am–9pm

› Roppongi station, exit 8

sadaharuaoki.jp

As futuristic as Tokyo is, the city always has an eye on the past, manifesting itself in old-world coffee houses known as kissaten, retro buildings and a plethora of vintage stores that sell everything from clothing to books and records, toys and more. Kissaten are a true Tokyo time-warp — old-school, independently owned cafes where coffee is made with great attention to detail and served in vintage china cups in quaint rooms soundtracked by mid-century jazz. As soon as you step into these time-stood-still cafes, you will be transported to simpler, gentler times.

Vintage stores are usually ramshackle affairs with piles of clothing teetering on the brink of collapse, every style and material covered, a rifle fest that could see you losing hours, even days. The majority of retro clothing on display is Americana, military wear and '50s styles. Retro toys and bookstores are treasure-troves of Japanese and Western delights and regular market stalls are laden with Japanese objet d'art from the distant and not-too-distant past. Vintage Japanese signage, LPs, tins and trinkets are ready to be unearthed and taken home to give your house that unique historical edge, telling their story with every dent, scuff or scratch.

You'll find vintage stores all over Tokyo, but if you want to spend a day in an area overrun with them, don't miss Shimokitazawa and Koenji, Akihabara for toys and Jimbocho for books. Each of these areas has a serious amount of vintage shopping opportunities. They also offer a fascinating glimpse into the past with places and spaces that recall the glory days of the Showa period (1926—89): mid-century enclaves with intriguing relics.

A quick note: many kissaten and small vintage stores, true to theme, have old-world values, so they are cash only.

TOKYO TIME WARP

東京物語

MONOZUKI
物豆奇

Nishi-Ogikubo

3-12-10 Nishiogi-Kita, Suginami-ku

Mon–Sun 11.30am–8pm

‣ Nishi-Ogikubo station, north exit

The first thing you'll notice about Monozuki is the arresting frontage which looks like a Horta designed, 1970s meets Belle Epoque church, strikingly out of place in the somewhat faceless suburban backstreet façades of Nishi-Ogikubo. The stained-glass windows cast a reverential light in this chapel to coffee. Established in 1975, the interior features thick wood accents on the walls, floors, tables and furniture, and the low clusters of yellow lamps and floor tiles in muted brown perfectly evoke the '70s. It resembles a large cuckoo clock that is actually full of smaller cuckoo clocks (and various pendulum clocks for variety). Most of the clocks have stopped at different times, giving you a sense that you have stepped back, forward and sideways in time, and this feeling continues with the soft jazz which soundtracks some of Tokyo's best black coffee. Sweet accompaniments are almost an afterthought in a place where coffee is the star (even the most basic blend is a memorable mash-up of mocha, Colombia, Brazil, and Mandheling) and will be lovingly crafted while you admire the chunky Irori fireplace. Michelle also highly recommends the matcha iced-latte topped off with a dollop of ice-cream.

COFFEE HOUSE POEM
コーヒー専門店ぽえむ

Koenji

4-44-5 Koenji, Suginami-ku

Mon–Sun 9am–11pm

‣ Koenji station, south exit

nikkahan.co.jp

Established in 1961, Poem is more 'Beat' than haiku – more Kerouac than Basho and more bohemian than barista. The vintage yellow entrance sign sets the mood, leading you into a cosy space where a youthful staff bring an edgy update to the classic, old-school Japanese coffee house. Pork pie hats, tattoos, Bob Dylan T-shirts and pencil and pad are recommended accessories. The tables have coffee beans layered under the glass table tops and well-worn mustard and brown benches line the wall; furniture with stories to tell. Peace and love are still on the menu along with cheese toast, chiffon cake, hashed beef and rice and an extensive range of tempting scones. The coffee is classic pour-over, the soundtrack rock and roll, blues and soul. Grab a table and scribble away the afternoon, perhaps composing a poetic ode to the charm of this popular Koenji afternoon hangout.

KAYABA COFFEE
カヤバ珈琲

Yanaka

6-1-29 Yanaka, Taito-ku
Tues–Sun 8am–6pm
‣ Nezu station, exit 1

The northern tip of Ueno park (*see* p. 67) gives way to quiet, strollable backstreets and it's here that you'll find Kayaba, a cafe dating back to 1938, making it one of Tokyo's very first kissaten (vintage coffee house). Set to close in 2006, the local Taito Historical Society stepped in and 2008 saw a revival of the cafe's fortunes. History is written over the exterior, a stunning two-storey dark wood and brick frontage with an instantly recognisable yellow sign. The upstairs tatami room hints of the glory days of this atmospheric cafe. Sit cross-legged before the low tables and gaze out of the ample windows while feasting on a morning set of juice, coffee, egg sandwiches and salad. Or why not make like a local and order the red bean butter toast? It's the perfect spot to while away the afternoon with cake, parfaits or the kissaten's specialty, as proclaimed on the yellow sign: anmitsu (red bean, agar jelly and fruit), made for a lazy summer afternoon. The most popular coffee here is The Russian but house blends and international roasts are also delicious.

PAULISTA
カフェーパウリスタ

Ginza

Nagasaki Center building 1F, 8-9 Ginza, Chuo-ku

Mon–Fri 9am–8pm, Sat 9am–7.30pm, Sun 11.30am–7pm

‣ Ginza station, exit A1

paulista.co.jp

Established around 1911, Paulista is thought to be one of the first, if not the very first, kissaten (vintage coffee house) in Japan. Its home since 1970, on swanky Ginza's main street Chuo-dori, adds to its status as an iconic cafe. The legendary status is further confirmed by the booth with the memorial photograph to John and Yoko, who used to frequent the establishment (further commemorated with a signature cup and saucer set). Try to grab this booth to soak up the vintages vibes while admiring the highly polished floors, warm woods, brass and chandeliers that give Paulista an upmarket feel. The classic kissaten menu is a little more expansive than at many other kissaten and includes breakfast sets of house-blend coffee and pancakes or 'big' thickly cut toast, salad and, if it takes your fancy, eggs or wieners – quirky east-meets-low-brow-west fare in that unique kissaten style. Quiche, cheese toast, hot dogs and curry give way to afternoon indulgences of parfait and cake. Coffee types range from local organic blends to popular South American beans, all of which can be bought instore to take home and re-create that rich Paulista flavour.

CAFÉ DE L'AMBRE
カフェ・ド・ランブル

Ginza

8-10-15 Ginza, Chuo-ku

Mon–Sun 11am–8pm

‣ Shinsaibashi station, exit 1

cafedelambre.com

In operation since 1948, this ultra-smooth kissaten (vintage coffee house) captures the very spirit of mid-century Ginza, a town on the rise, populated by chic and affluent Tokyo-ites who wanted to smoke and drink coffee while talking about the latest styles in music and fashion. It was a time when Western influence brought American '50s style to Japan. Men dressed in sharp suits and had slicked-back hair while the women's moga (modern girl) style from the '20s and '30s evolved into a new and independent sophistication and women sported bob haircuts and vibrantly patterned kimono or sharp-yet-casual Western dress. The cafe's dark, moody enclave with European-style coffee and petite desserts is soundtracked by cool jazz. We love to laze an afternoon away here, soaking in this Showa period (1926–89) joie de vivre, while enjoying their superb coffee jelly, a tiny delight in a shallow vintage dessert glass accompanied by a blob of cream. Owner Ichiro Sekiguchi was there from the beginning and was still working in the cafe until he passed away at 104.

COFFEE TIMES
珈琲タイムス

Shinjuku

3-35-11 Shinjuku, Shinjuku-ku
Mon–Sat 8am–10pm,
Sun 8am–9pm
‣ Shinjuku station, exit E9
times1967.com

Relive late '60s Japan when you could sit back with a coffee, light up a cigarette and read the Shinbun (newspaper) to get your dose of daily events. Coffee Times opened in 1967 and stands firmly as a Showa period (1926–89) bastion against the encroachment of towering skyscrapers and getting your news on your smartphone. A mix of early risers, book nerds, kids on dates and people who haven't slept, populate Coffee Times in the morning, sipping expertly made drip coffee. Dark wood furniture, red velvet booths and thick beams warm up exposed brick walls, while medieval chic plays out in wrought-iron chandeliers and curios placed randomly on the copper tables which stand on '70s brown slate-tile floors. Older clientele come here to pretend that things haven't moved on and kids come here to feel what it was like when their parents were dating. The soundtrack of slow jazz and bossa nova has 'Fly Me to The Moon' and 'I've Got You Under My Skin' on high rotation. Big toast and boiled eggs accompany café au lait, Americano, a house blend or a melon cream soda, or in the afternoons order cheesecake, sandwiches or a spaghetti Napolitan (Japanese ketchup spaghetti) or carbonara. As always, the coffee jelly is a must have.

KISSATEN GALANT
喫茶店ギャラン

Ueno

6-14-4 Ueno, Taito-ku
Mon–Sun 8am–10.30pm
‣ Ueno station, exit 3

Galant resolutely wears the late Showa period (1926–89) on its sleeve and relives the glory days of the '70s by peacocking its unabashedly glitzy and gaudy interior. Dating to 1977, the flare of the era is apparent in every element of the furnishing, signage and décor right down to the music – a mix of jazz, lounge and hits from the '60s to the '80s. The staff uniforms are checked red and white retro chic. The menu probably hasn't changed in forever and the kissaten (vintage coffee house) staples of large toast and salad sets, egg toast and omuraisu (rice-filled omelette) are amped up with touches like bacon and cheese. The desserts are suitably over the top – towering parfaits, soda floats and generous slices of cake, making this spot perfect for morning coffee or afternoon dates over a chocolate and mikan parfait or lurid green ice-cream float. Coffee is the usual kissaten staple of house blend, Americano, espresso and lattes. There is a hint of retro futurism in the décor and a clash of patterned tiled floors, vibrant leather couches and brown brick walls are all hinted at in the delightfully chintzy exterior. So, slip on your flares, a colourful shirt and order up a mentaiko pasta or a curry with an iced-coffee or juice. Everything old is new again.

TRAVELLER'S NOTE

In keeping with the décor, and the retro vibes, it's cash only at Coffee Times.

DESIGN NOTE

The women's bathroom at Kissaten Galant is a wonderful timepiece of floral pale pink tiles.

OPEN
Cafe

CHATEI HATOU
茶亭 羽當

Shibuya

1-15-19 Shibuya, Shibuya-ku
Mon–Sun 11am–11.30pm
‣ Shibuya station, exit B4

When you step into Chatei Hatou kissaten (vintage coffee house), time stands still and the world outside melts away. The interior is a cosy mishmash of European antiques, dark wood and Chinese design, with low lighting and classical music adding to the days-of-yore allure. You won't be getting latte art here, but you will get a warm welcome from genial host Toyoshi Taguchi who has been working at Chatei Hatou since 1989. He'll size you up as you take your seat and then choose a cup to suit your personality from the 'great wall of china' behind him. Michelle's cup design was an illustrated sunflower, so he definitely captured her essence, while the reading of Steve's mostly plain cup design was a little more obscure ... but we were mesmerised as we watched him make the coffee, a master craftsman in action. Order some fluffy chiffon cake with maple icing as the ideal accompaniment to your brew. You're paying for the perfect blend in an exquisite cup in a beautiful setting here so you might find it a little pricier than usual, but it is a thoroughly unique Tokyo experience.

YURIA PEMUPERU
ゆりあぺむぺる

Kichijoji

1-1-6 Musashino, Kichijoji Minamicho
Tues–Sun 11.30am–8pm
‣ Kichijoji station, west or south gate

An enduringly popular kissaten (vintage coffee house) founded in 1976, with a lazy afternoon feel that sits in stark contrast to the over-the-top styling of its interior, Yuria Pemuperu offers coffee and cake and a yoshoku menu (Japanese spins on Western-style dishes), such as pasta, curry, pizza and egg sandwiches. However, it's the oversized cream soda floats in pop colours that draw the crowds. Sip your luridly coloured soda (choose from red, blue or green) while admiring the mishmash of European style antique décor, art nouveau and an oddball mix of vintage knick-knacks, lamps, chandeliers, plants and 'distressed' wood cabinets. The best seats are the upstairs or downstairs bay window booths where you can happily eat your excellent coffee jelly while watching the Kichijoji shoppers stroll by. They also make cocktails and arrange cocktail parties if you feel like inviting some friends (bookings essential).

WHISTLER/ CHART

ウィスラー／チャート

Koenji

4-30-8 Koenjiminami, Suginami-ku

Mon–Sun 12–9pm

‣ Koenji station, south exit

ameblo.jp/whistler-and-chart

This twin retro store caters to many styles and you won't have any trouble putting together a stylishly vintage outfit from clothes that sit on groaning racks and shelves. However, Whistler/Chart have a much more alluring point of difference: racks and racks of pre-loved shoes. Walls of boots and brogues, loafers and espadrilles will have you investigating quality and size for hours, hunting out the perfect pair of Oxfords or trainers. Casual shoes are piled high on shelves and stuffed into jumbles in boxes. Downstairs, American and European fashions are on show, 'trad' as the Japanese call it, while upstairs a more casual mix can be found, with active wear and military garb available – with over 20 years in the business these attached vintage stores know their stock. Like most vintage stores in Tokyo, you'll find plenty of Amekaji, the Japanese obsession with (and reinterpretation of) American casual fashion that will provide you with plenty of pieces to help put together contemporary outfits.

AREA NOTE

Whistler/Chart is a good first stop in Koenji, but just a tip of the pre-loved iceberg in this town. Make sure you also visit **Lover Soul**, **Hurry Up**, **Super Old** and **Atlantis** and for vinyl, **Be In Record** (*see* p. 171).

BIG TIME
ビッグタイム

Shimokitazawa

2-26-15 Kitazawa, Setagaya-ku

Mon–Thurs 11am–8pm, Fri–Sun 11am–9pm

‣ Shimokitazawa station, west exit northside

bigtime.jp

Vintage clothes shopping is an extreme sport in Shimokitazawa and Big Time is one of the most popular stores. Excellent vintage from the 1950s to the 1990s, from Europe and America, is sourced by the store's buyers and arranged neatly onto groaning racks and shelves, or stuffed haphazardly into boxes and crates. If you're looking for clothing from the '50s, '60s or '70s that is in superb condition for its age, you have definitely come to the right place. Finally! You can strut down the street in that Hawaiian, bowling or '90s grunge flannel shirt like you've always wanted. Everything is cyclic right? There is an extensive range of accessories at Big Time as well, so throw together a pork pie hat with a tutu and some costume jewellery and invent something new from everything old. There is plenty of vintage shopping to be done around here. Don't miss our favourites, **Little Trip To Heaven**, **Flamingo** and **Trefacstyle**. For vintage vinyl, head to **City Country City** (*see* p. 172).

OKUNO BUILDING
奥野ビル

Ginza

1-9-8 Ginza, Chuo-ku

Check ahead for individual business opening hours

‣ Ginza-itchome station, exit A10

Designed by architect Kawamoto Ryōichi and built as a luxury apartment in 1932, the Okuno Building was originally called the Ginza Apartments. It holds a significant place in Tokyo's cultural history as a refuge for artists and free-thinkers during a time of societal unrest in the 1960s and stands in stark contrast to its surroundings in Ginza, looking out of place in the best possible way, and retaining much of its nostalgic charm. You instantly feel the building's eclectic appeal upon entering. Take a moment to explore the mailboxes and note the various business names and logos. With 70 rooms to discover, you could spend the day unearthing treasures. The interior is full of character, with crumbling walls, a manual elevator and an authentic patina that tells the story of its past. If only the walls could talk, the salons and gatherings that once took place here would come to life. The 1st floor is dedicated to antique shops, whilst floors 2 through 6 house galleries and private businesses. On the 6th of each month, visitors can peek inside Apartment 306, a Showa period (1926–89) hair salon once owned by Suda Yoshi. A resident for decades, Yoshi continued to live there after her salon closed, passing away in 2009 at the age of 100. Imagine the vibrant conversations she had, the fashion she wore, the music she listened to, and the stories of her clientele!

VINTAGE, FLEA & JUNK MARKETS
骨董市と蚤の市

Lovers of vintage, antique or tatty treasures may want to plan their trip according to the Tokyo vintage market schedule. With large-scale events in carparks, parks and shrines, markets pop up and live their best life before everything is packed up with extreme precision, leaving the space once occupied with merriment, bargaining, food stalls and a festive atmosphere, empty, but full of promise. We love sifting through the vintage markets, and have found some really special and surprising things. Expect pre-loved kimono, obi (sash), yukata (summer kimono), textiles (including boro and sashiko stitched), furniture, Kokeshi and Daruma dolls, ceramics, hair combs, washi paper, iron teapots, chawan (matcha bowl), baskets, calligraphy brushes, woodblock prints, coins, tools and more. Flea market fare includes toys, magazines, vintage vinyl and poster paraphernalia, manga, tins, prints and magazines.

Perennial favourite **Oedo Antique Market** (Yurakucho station, Tokyo International Forum exit) is held every first and third Sunday at the Tokyo International Forum, and is just near Tokyo Station. It is populated by 250-plus stalls, some run by real characters who have had stalls at the market for many years. They also hold a market at Yoyogi park on random dates.

Tokyo's oldest market **Setagaya Boroichi Market** (Setagaya or Kamimachi stations) features 700 sprawling stalls along Boroichi St. Now enshrined with the title of an Intangible Folk Cultural Property, the event was started in 1578 by clan leader and feudal lord Hojo Ujimasa. A vast and varied range of items are sold at the market. The term 'junk market or rag fair' by Japanese standards is more like a wondrous festival of outdoor curios to us.

Harajuku Yoyogi Flea Market (Harajuku station, Takeshita-dori exit) advertises proudly that it is a household-waste-only market, as does **Mottainai Market** ('mottainai' can be translated as 'don't waste it'), which mysteriously changes venues, times and dates for each event. Their commitment to giving new life to items no longer used has struck a chord with eco Tokyo-ites and visitors alike.

Heiwajima Antique Fair is held four or five times a year and runs for three days at the Heiwajima Ryutsu Center building (Ryutsu Center station). It specialises more in traditional antiques than just flea market fare.

TRAVELLER'S NOTE

As usual, if weather is extreme, it's likely the markets will be cancelled. This does not apply to the **Heiwajima Antique Fair** which is held indoors.

As it moved into the late 20th century, a high disposable income and a rise in consumer goods meant that Japan became synonymous with consumer culture. Fashion styles updated weekly, everything came wrapped in plastic packaging and the trend was towards a love for new and often unneeded things. However, late into the 2010s and in particular, post Covid, Japan's collective thinking has made a sizeable shift to the future of the planet and its overall health and wellbeing. A new breed of store has evolved, fighting against waste and using traditional techniques, as well as contemporary know-how, to create a more sustainable and eco-friendly shopping experience.

To shop sustainably in Tokyo, we recommend buying food from organic markets and buying gifts from local makers, flea markets or second-hand stores. Think carefully about what you choose to bring home. Purchasing well-thought-out vintage gifts with personality will delight loved ones. Some ideas include handmade pottery, kitchenalia, vintage kimono and old photos.

As you plan your trip to Tokyo, consider packing only what you need. Hand-luggage trips are not as hard as they may seem (we always travel with just hand luggage). Packing this way means you can move around more freely, and you are not encumbered by your luggage. We recommend that you take the following items to Japan and as you travel around Tokyo too: a collapsible food storage container for any leftovers, a hot drink flask/cup, a water bottle with filter (fill with green tea or water each day), and a cotton or linen tote bag for carrying your rubbish (bins can be hard to find) and for all that shopping.

When you're selecting your accommodation, choose accommodation that fits your values. There are options for green accommodation in Tokyo on most booking sites. You can even choose a room with an eco-plan, which can mean less room cleaning and sheet washing.

Thankfully, Tokyo is also becoming more eco conscious in its building design and sustainable transport, too.

TOKYO

東京物語

ECO

SUSTAINABLE BUILDING
サステナブル建築

Tokyo's commitment to the environment continues to play out in its 'Carbon Half' plan which aims to cut emissions in half by 2030, and the 'Zero Emissions by 2050' directive. All new houses built from 2025 must have solar panels, and the construction of more 'passive housing' and sustainable energy practices are now the norm rather than an experimental idea. New shopping centre construction and rural development projects have green spaces that use nature to balance emissions, like the **Meguro Sky Garden** (*see* p. 144) and skyscraper design that is mindful of eco practices both during construction and once they have opened. In a short time, Tokyo has become a leader in the field of sustainable practice. Many of Tokyo's buildings adopt sustainability in both small, everyday ways and in larger ways which are changing the face of how we save the planet.

To see this in action, visit the rooftop of **Ginza Six**, **Parco Rooftop Garden** in Shibuya, **Artre Rooftop Garden** in Ebisu and **Tokyu Plaza Harakado** and **Tokyu Plaza Omotesando Omokado** in Harajuku, to name a few.

TOKYO RIVERSIDE DISTILLERY
東京リバーサイド蒸溜所

Kuramae

3-9-1 Kuramae, Taito-ku
Mon–Sun 1–7pm
‣ Kuramae station, exit A6
shop.ethicalspirits.jp

Craft gin dispensed through a hole-in-the-wall bar in breezy Kuramae? Tokyo Riverside Distillery certainly ticks all the boxes for the gin aficionado and it has the added cachet of having the gin still set up on the premises as well as the eco credentials of being made under the banner of the Ethical Spirits Company. Pop by in an afternoon to purchase a bottle of their handmade gin, described as 'regenerative gin', which uses ethical nutrients and practices. It certainly revives the tired wanderer, but here the word 'regenerative' describes a process where nothing is wasted and everything that can be used in the crafting of the gin will be used, creating a kind of cycle of life where the distillery uses eco practices to replenish itself. Tokyo Riverside Distillery strive to bring out the 'hidden gem' of the gin, a unique flavour that both evokes a feeling of nostalgia while moving the flavour profile of gin forward. The open window dispenses the gin in a 'street bar' setup, so order yourself a glass while watching local Kuramae go about its daily business. While you are there, take a sneak peek through the side window at the gin still and smell the hint of juniper berries upon the air. A small bar upstairs serves food to complement the gin tastings. You can also book a tour, which unveils the ethical distilling process to the eco curious.

SUSTAINABLE NOTE

DAMDAM are committed to reducing carbon dioxide in their factories by 10 per cent per year and 1 per cent of profits are invested back into local community organisations.

DAMDAM
ダムダム

Harajuku

4-9-5 Jingumae, Shibuya-ku
Mon–Sun 11am–7pm
‣ Omotesando station, exit A2
damdamtokyo.com

Tokyo clean beauty brand DAMDAM is gaining eco momentum, producing organic products using classic Japanese ingredients. Housed in a minimalist white box on the backstreets of Omotesando, their plant-based products include skincare, haircare and self-care items such as natural face cloths and the Kassa face sculpture tool. DAMDAM products are cruelty free with organic certifications, 100 per cent recyclable packaging, and take care to use non-toxic paper and ink and responsibly sourced packaging materials. Perfect for sensitive skin, DAMDAM use unique ingredients such as Japanese rice, snow mushrooms and salt, cloud glove and shiso (Japanese basil) in products like their popular Mochi Mochi Luminous Cream, Silk Rice Cleansing Oil, Snow Mushroom Salt Cleanser, award-winning Citrus Glow Serum and shiso shampoo and conditioner. Hair products come with refills and innovative self-sealing boxes. The interior of the store is inspired by Japanese culture and artisan practices. The stone floor is influenced by Japanese gardens, and joinery is made from washi, wood and lacquer. The Meli Melo and Amber Incense are amongst our store favourites, as are the stunning incense holders, designed by Imada Tomoyuki using salvaged wood from storm disasters.

ONLINE STORES & BRANDS
オンラインストア&ブランド

From early on in Japan's history, repurposing and reinventing clothing and objects has been standard practice. Tokyo has taken this idea of 'mottainai', essentially meaning 'what a waste', and applied it to clothing and consumer goods, using leftover product in new and inventive ways and making sure that things are recycled rather than replaced. If you're looking for repurposed goods and innovative design, plus you don't want to carry much in your luggage, these stores are online only. **Plasticity** don't have a physical store but you can purchase clothes upcycled from old umbrellas. **Ichie Ichie** makes accessories like bags, wallets and purses from repurposed obi sashes. **Newsed** take would-be-trash and convert it into usable household items and jewellery. Likewise, **I was a Kimono** make clothes from repurposed vintage kimono. Even if you're not travelling to Tokyo, you can experience the city's commitment to sustainability through these brands.

ORGANIC MARKETS
オーガニックマーケット

To save money and shop sustainably in Tokyo, head to the food markets. They are great for sampling local cuisine and seeing the neighbourhood go about its everyday living. A wonderful range of freshly picked organic produce awaits at **Ark Hills Marche** (Tameike station, exit 13) in Roppongi. Held in the Ark Karajan Plaza in Ark Hills complex every Saturday (and sometimes on a Tuesday), the market is a colourful mix of tented stalls with a festive atmosphere, including music, food trucks and produce delivered direct by farmers from prefectures all over Japan. With a motto of 'a marche where you can meet the producers', the happy chit chat between growers and buyers makes for an authentic experience where you can feel the love and passion behind cultivating produce with care and with sustainability in mind. Note: the market will proceed if it is raining but may be cancelled in extreme weather, so check ahead.

Another market on our Tokyo list is **Aoyama Farmers Market at UNU** (Omotesando station, exit b2), known for its organic farm produce and craft coffee. Popping up every weekend, the market is a relaxed and colourful affair, making busy Aoyama-dori suddenly seem like a country setting. Tents and stalls are set up in the forum-like space in front of the United Nations University building and across vast Aoyama-dori directly opposite sprawling Aoyama Gakuin University. With a mantra of 'we are what we eat', the farmers market offers stalls selling freshly picked farm-grown produce. Think of the freshest strawberries, homemade muffins with organic ingredients, organic chocolate and natural wines. There is also an antique market at **Ark Hills** that is held on the fourth Sunday of every month.

DESIGN NOTE
The dotted circle 'tambourine' signature print is a timeless minä design that is effortlessly beautiful adorning fabric, crockery and other coveted items.

MINÄ PERHONEN
ミナペルホネン

Daikanyama

Hillside Terrace 102/103, 18-12 Sarugakucho, Shibuya-ku

Mon–Sun 12–8pm

‣ Daikanyama station, central exit

mina-perhonen.jp

The Daikanyama branch of minä perhonen's store is a must-visit for fans of Akira Minagawa's wistful clothing made from his exquisite and, at times, boldly graphic textiles. Translating as 'I, Butterfly' from the Finnish language (Minagawa has a deep connection with Finland), his creations are as much art as they are fashion. His brand, which began in 1995 (but wasn't named minä perhonen until 2003), always had a close link to craft, the handmade and sustainable practices. In Minagawa's very first designs (when he left a job working part-time at a fish market to concentrate on his art), recycled material and fabric remnants were used to construct playful and alluring pieces, which mimicked the spirit of the timeless beauty of a butterfly's wing. Designs are made to last, with signature shapes and fabrics remodelled and reimagined subtly throughout successive collections. minä is a slow-fashion brand coveted by anyone obsessed with fabric creation, print techniques and meticulous and intricate textiles. Float through the flagship boutique, where the warm woods and the small graphic details on fabric walls are the perfect environment for the elegant clothes. A visit to minä perhonen's lifestyle store **Call**, in Aoyama, is also a must.

MEGURO SKY GARDEN
目黒天空庭園

Meguro

9F, 1-9-2 Ohashi, Meguro-ku

Mon–Sun 7am–9pm

‣ Ikejiri Ohashi station, east exit

If you're near Shibuya station an hour before sunset, jump on the semi express Den-en-toshi line to Ikejiri Ohashi station and watch the sun set from an urban oasis, high above the bustling city. Meguro Sky Garden was built by the Tokyu train company, who have made a commitment to decarbonisation, renewables and recycling. The eco-conscious 'rooftop lid' garden sits atop the Hashi motorway junction, a bold project beautifying an ugly freeway, absorbing carbon dioxide and providing a verdant green space for locals. Winner of multiple design, eco and urban park awards, it literally brings the temperature of the area down, as well as improves air quality. What would normally be an eyesore has been transformed into an urban oasis with planning and architectural teams using the shapes of the freeways and integrating them into the design of the circuit-style garden. Along a circular path, 11 concept spaces unfold, each with significant, themed plantings. There are over 1000 plants including cherry blossoms, large-scale tortured pines in pots and seasonal shrubs and blooms. Zoned areas include community veggie boxes, a Japanese garden and picnic tables. As an added bonus, a distant neighbour, Mount Fuji, reveals itself to lucky garden visitors on clear days.

TRAVELLER'S NOTE

The Sky Garden can be closed in extreme weather.

SUSTAINABLE TRAVEL
環境にやさしい歩き方

There are many small things you can do on your Tokyo trip to help the planet, reduce your carbon footprint and make ethical exchanges.

Where possible, eat at small businesses, and buy food at markets, food trucks and stalls. Try local organic sake or shochu (distilled spirit) and craft beers to support local; eat less meat and fish or eat sustainably sourced meat from small businesses. **Tsukiji Outer Market** (*see* p. 94), **Aoyama Farmers Market** and other organic markets (*see* p. 142) are great options for fresh food experiences, and Tokyo has many wonderful festivals, all of which include pop-up food stalls.

Another way you can immerse yourself in the local culture and travel sustainably at the same time is to do a class on something cultural run by a local craftsperson; see **Pigment** (*see* p. 54), **Kuge Crafts** (*see* p. 16) and **Sogetsu** (*see* p. 44) for workshops.

Bins can sometimes be hard to find on the streets of Tokyo, so carry a small bag to store waste until you can dispose of it. The municipal bin system in Tokyo is colour-coded, so make sure you discard of your waste in the right bin.

SUSTAINABLE TRANSPORT
環境にやさしい移動手段

Tokyo is a wonderful city to explore on foot so choose a destination for a morning stroll, catch a train there, then get your steps up by walking around. The city's train network is excellent and travelling on trains uses around five times less carbon than travelling by car. Tokyu Railways has made a strong sustainable statement by committing to using alternative green renewable power sources, including solar and hydro power for all of its trains. If you are particularly interested in eco design, head to the Odakyu stations that have been built with environmental factors in mind (Higashi-Kitazawa, Shimokitazawa, and Setagaya-daita stations).

The bus network around Tokyo can be harder to work out than the trains, but many buses are now low-emission vehicles (electric and fuel cell buses). Cycling certain parts of the city can be another way to explore Tokyo sustainably. **Yoyogi park** is a friendly and fun cycling experience, perfect for beginner riders and families (you can hire tandem and kids' bikes here). Jump off the train at Yoyogi Hachiman station, then head over to **Yoyogi Park Cycle Center** to hire your bike for the day. The sprawling park features sakura (cherry blossoms) in season and a ginkgo (ancient tree) avenue in autumn, as well as spaces for cycling, jogging, picnicking and strolling.

BIKE HIRE NOTE

Many accommodations in Tokyo now have bikes to hire or if cycling is your priority, download the **Hello Cycling!** app. One of our favourite places to hire a bike is **Tokyo Bike**; it has gorgeous bikes, fantastic locations to hire from, and we love to ride these bikes around the neighbourhood streets (we also own these bikes at home). You'll find stores in Yanaka, Nakameguro, Kichijoji and Gotokuji; opening hours vary (tokyobike.com/tokyobikerentals).

KAPITAL
キャピタル

Ebisu

2-20-2 Ebisu-Minami, Shibuya-ku

Mon–Sun 11am–8pm

› Ebisu station, west exit

kapital.jp

The traditional craft of boromono (meaning 'rags'), repurposing quality indigo-dyed fabrics and layering sashiko stitching to create wearable, eclectic fashion, is Kapital's mantra. The attention to detail with the materials and craftsmanship is renowned. Walking into the store, you can feel the revolutionary spirit. It's a defiant movement, fixed on the reinvention and re-use of fabric as a means of sustainability, but also as a means of inspiration and creativity. Denim is upcycled (it's no surprise that Kapital was born in Okayama's denim district, Kojima), as are vintage American fabrics, army greens and pre- and postwar materials, using boro techniques to construct and reconstruct using offcuts, or repairing and reimagining tattered pre-loved clothing. The result is playful and curious, and often the clothes appear tribal or native, as befits the repurposed, handmade aesthetic. The interior is decked out with odd memorabilia and twisted displays, army surplus and oddball sculptures that might look better off in an amusement park ghost house. It's a quirky experience, yet Tokyo ingenuity manages to meld the chic and the bizarre to create something new and contemporary and, at times, surprisingly luxe and even catwalk ready.

By day, Tokyo is an astounding array of cultural experiences, sights and sounds, with adventures around every corner and seemingly endless new discoveries. At night however, some of Tokyo's more faceless buildings and streets suddenly come to life — lights flicker on creating neon streetscapes, roller blinds unfurl revealing tiny standing bars, and lanterns light up along alleys and laneways with characterful long-standing eateries and late-night ramen joints.

There are plenty of options for bar hopping, relaxing to the best tunes and gazing in admiration at vast record collections and absurdly elaborate sound system set-ups in the city's listening bars. From atmospheric yokocho (alleyways), drinking dens and late-night shopping, Tokyo at night is a world unto itself and an endless opportunity for new experiences and some excellent night photography.

It's not all drinking and shopping however, you can also get in touch with your spiritual side by visiting a shrine or temple late at night, illuminated, atmospheric and tranquil.

Plan at least a few nights to stay up and immerse yourself in the Tokyo wonderland of your imagination as it suddenly flickers into reality.

TOKYO

東京物語

NOIR

AMEYA YOKOCHO
アメヤ横丁

Ueno

‣ **Ueno station, Shinobazu exit**

Springing up in the black market years after World War II, the narrow winding alleys beneath the elevated train tracks between Ueno and Okachimachi stations are noisy, crowded and wear their seedy charm with pride. There's definitely still a hint of the underground at Ameya Yokocho, with each stall and bar having an air of the speakeasy about it, but amongst the flea market tat and novelty souvenirs you'll find fresh food stalls that can more than supply your feast for a picnic in nearby Ueno park (*see* p. 67). Alternately, slide yourself into one of the many inexpensive yakitori, tempura or ramen joints and sample some seafood, which the market is known for. Food carts, standing bars and eateries are crammed into every available niche, ensuring no real estate goes to waste. It's open during the day but at night it seems to transform, so take a seat in any joint that takes your fancy and order beer and whatever else is going, and settle in for some people watching; odds are you'll see something going on somewhere to which you'll need to turn a blind eye. Diamonds in the rough? Try **Gyukatsu Motomura** (2F, 4-10-17 Ueno, Taito-ku) for tonkatsu (crumbed pork cutlet) and **UO KUSA** (6-10-7 Ueno, Taito-ku) for sushi and sashimi.

AREA NOTE
Long-standing **Kissaten Galant** (*see* p. 128) is perfect for an afternoon cream soda and cake before heading into the eateries and bars.

NONBEI YOKOCHO
のんべい横丁

Shibuya

‣ Shibuya station, Hachiko exit

Wedged between Miyashita park and the craziness of the labyrinthine Shibuya station, you'll find a little pocket of calm, a shanty town of teeny-tiny bars and eateries squeezed into two picturesque, historic lamp-lit alleyways. Some of the bars only hold a total of six people at a time, while others are spread over two floors, but even in the bigger places the most petite person will wonder if they'll be able to squeeze up the pokey staircases or wedge themselves into the counter seat. Drinking and stories are what you've come for however, and you'll feel the hospitality of days gone by at these long-standing bars. The drinks will be accompanied by excellent food as well, and you'll find everything from yakitori restaurants to home-style cooking, just like a salaryman's mum used to make. Nonbei is slang for 'drunkard' so don't be shy – squash yourself into this delightful Tokyo time warp and drink to '50s and '60s Tokyo.

HARMONICA YOKOCHO
ハモニカ横丁

Kichijoji

‣ Kichijoji station, north exit

Located to the left of **Sun Road Arcade** (*see* p. xxxii) in Kichijoji, you'll find the entrance to one of Tokyo's most atmospheric and authentic yokocho (alleyway). The small rabbit warren of restaurants and bars (Harmonica Yokocho is named because it resembles the reeds of a harmonica in its layout) retains the atmosphere of the flea market it once was during World War II. You can still get some vintage finds here, but mostly you'll come to eat and drink, lazily wandering from one tiny bar or eatery to another, most of which are open rooms looking onto the narrow-covered alleys. Graze on yakitori, gyoza or noodles while guzzling, that is, responsibly sipping well-priced booze, and engaging in friendly banter with the store owners. It's best at night, when the plethora of vintage signs light up, red lanterns glow and the chatter is at its most ebullient. As usual, there as some true gems to be winkled out. Try **Minmin** for gyoza and tasty sushi and sashimi at **Katakuchi**.

GADO-SHITA
ガード下

Yurakucho

‣ Yurakucho station, Hibiya or central west exit

From Shinbashi to Yurakucho stations, and Yurakucho to Tokyo stations, you'll find the Gado-Shita (under the girders), a row of eateries set in the stone walls beneath the railway tracks; they're open to the street and the Yurakucho station exits will take you right there. Atmospheric, especially at night when the lamps light up, these small spaces are perfect for a boozy night out. Standing bars, gyoza specialists, yakitori joints and European specialist eateries that provide everything from Italian pasta and pizza to German bratwurst and schnitzel, can be found bubbling with life along the strip. Takeaway food can be ordered at hole-in-the-wall joints along the way and ramshackle eateries (with a happy hour that goes on for several hours) make up an eco-system brimming with good cheer. Start at **Yurakucho Concourse** (3-5-1 Yurakucho, Chiyoda-ku), popping in to **Manpuku Shokudo** (2-4-1 Yurakucho, Chiyoda-ku) for beer and chips before wending your way towards the mega Tokyo Station (*see* p. xix), popping into whatever looks good, stopping to order some skewers at an izakaya (pubs with small plate food) and eating them with a highball or two while the trains rumble above you. A quintessential Tokyo experience that thankfully still retains all of its boisterous, proletarian charm.

日本

Side Show
丹下左膳

新橋ガード下横丁
SHINBASHI-YOKOCHO
横丁入口
入口

EBISU YOKOCHO
恵比寿横丁

Ebisu

1-7-4 Ebisu-Minami, Shibuya-ku

Sun–Mon 5pm–5am

‣ Ebisu station, east exit

ebisu-yokocho.com

At night Ebisu comes alive, roller doors reveal secret canteens and hidden eateries and grills start to sizzle and smoke. Workers and commuters flood into the area seeking to appease their hunger. Ebisu Yokocho is the distilling of that mad magic – a market space of separate bars and restaurants, elbow-to-elbow crowds drinking, eating, laughing and essentially just having the best, messiest time they can. This was where the old Yamashita 'shopping centre' used to thrive. Now it's a mishmash of Japanese-, Chinese- and even French-style bars where you can mix it up with locals until bleary eyed, you find yourselves staggering through Ebisu with street sweepers and early risers for company.

TATEMICHIYA
立道屋

Daikanyama

B1F, 30-8 Sarugakucho, Shibuya-ku

Mon–Sat 6pm–12am

‣ Daikanyama station, east exit

'Hey Ho, Let's Go!' The fun kicks off at night in this grungy izakaya (pub with small plate food), a magnet for provocative, art conscious locals, hang-abouts and rock-and-roll diehards. Expect posters of the Sex Pistols, the Ramones and a soundtrack of punk, rock and punk rock, turned up to 11. Pop artist Yoshitomo Nara loves it here, and has scribbled illustrations on the walls and outside on the top of the stairs at the street entrance. Also don't miss Mick Jagger's signature near the entrance, although staff are likely to proudly point this out to you as you leave. The honest izakaya fare includes delicious, generously sized yakitori skewers and an atsuage (deep fried tofu) that people cross town for. Be brave and add some natto (fermented soybeans) to your meal – you'll either hate or handle this stinky bean but you should get some admiring looks for your commitment. Your host will be happily singing along to the music while he pours you something called a 'danger bomb' (you're only allowed three!) or a regional sake. Locals have their bottles lined up along the counter shelves. This izakaya is unpretentious and the food is delicious and, as a result, Daikanyama's cool kids and faded rockers come here in droves.

LATE NIGHT NOTE

Other notable yokocho include the popular **Omoide Yokocho** and **The Golden Gai** in Shinjuku.

TOTOROU
ととろう

Nakameguro

1-4-3 Kamimeguro, Meguro-ku

Mon–Fri 5pm–12am, Sat 4pm–12am, Sun 4–11pm

‣ Nakameguro station, west exit

In a quiet Nakameguro cul-de-sac you'll find a small, rustic and rowdy izakaya (pub with small plate food) presided over by the titular character from Studio Ghibli's *My Neighbor Totoro*. Though the furry creature doesn't loom large, you'll find him on glasses, mugs and lounging around on shelves generally soaking up the Nakameguro vibes. Young local staff happily pour drinks and serve wholesome rice bowls, grilled meat dishes and excellent sashimi. We rated the potato salad as well and although our vegetarian friends weren't fully catered for, they managed to find a few snacks to keep their drinks company. Cram yourself into a wooden booth and make a night of it or pop in after a walk along the canal. This den is open until midnight most nights so it's good for a mini late nighter and the drinks flow easily. Steve's go-to is a shochu highball and Michelle rated the lemon sour!

AKIRA
アキラ

Nakameguro

Riverside Terrace 106, 1-10-23 Nakameguro, Meguro-ku

Mon–Sun 5–11pm

‣ Nakameguro station, east exit

salt-group.jp/shop/akira_nakameguro

A hidden gem in a stunning repurposed machiya (traditional wooden townhouse) on a cul-de-sac overlooking the canal, Akira already has a lot going for it before you even get to the menu. The interior is elegant – traditional, pared back and comfortable with wooden tables and low-hung pendants – and the scent of smoke and grilled meats wafts over you on arrival. Grill your own meat at your table as you sit cross-legged on mats on the bamboo floor. Be adventurous and try the surprisingly delicious chicken tartare with ponzu sauce. Steve also recommends the crisped chicken skin, which is as delicious and wonderfully bad for you as it sounds. Make sure you book as it's popular and gets busy quickly, especially on the weekend. During hanami (cherry blossom season), the full flowering of the sakura (cherry blossom) gives Akira one of Tokyo's pinkest views, although getting in at this time would require a booking well in advance. Afterwards, why not walk along the Nakameguro canals, romantically lit up by lanterns, before heading into a bar for a nightcap or two.

LISTENING BARS
リスニングバー

If you know what year technics brought out the SL1200M2 turntable and know what a woofer or tweeter is, then pack your vintage headphones and sling your record bag over your shoulder, because when it comes to independent, underground listening bars, no city beats Tokyo. Your ultimate analogue listening night out is waiting in some of Tokyo's indie enclaves, especially Shimokitazawa, Shibuya, Koenji and Ebisu. Expect ramshackle shelves of vintage vinyl, retro record players, an enthusiastic, music loving host spinning the discs and late-night drinking hours. Specifically themed, you'll mostly find soul and jazz bars, sometimes combined, but there are also rock and roll, indie and heavy rock bars.

Head to Ginza for **Soul Dining Bar Ginza Magic** (Ginza station, exit A2). You'll find **Jazz Bar SOULTRANE** (the name says it all) in Asakusa (Asakusa station, main exit), and try out the all-night vibes of **Little Soul Café**, **music bar rpm** (Shinjuku-sanchome station, exit B2) and **Music Bar Rockaholic** (Shibuya station, Hachiko exit). Shibuya has a plethora of listening bars. **JBS** (Shibuya station, Hachiko exit) has an enviable vinyl collection and **Bar 33 /3** (Roppongi station, exit 5) leans towards rock with plenty of The Beatles. **Tangle** (Shibuya station, west exit) can be found on the 3rd floor of Shibuya Mark City and plays experimental jazz and rock. Just nearby you'll find the excellent **Blow Up. Music Bar-Cave** (Shibuya station, exit B1) has over 3000 records in an impressive collection selected by musician Takeshi Kobayashi. **RECORD BAR Analog** (Shibuya station, exit A0) in the love hotel district is a cool space, based on the Showa period (1926–89) snack bars. Also don't miss loungeroom-sized secret listening **Bar Otofuke** in Kiyosumi (Kiyosumi-Shirakawa station, exit A2).

JAZZ BAR SAMURAI
ジャズバーサムライ

Shinjuku

5F, 3-35-5 Shinjuku, Shinjuku-ku

Mon–Sun 6pm–1am

‣ Shinjuku station, south exit

You know you're in Tokyo when you get out of the elevator on the 5th floor of a random building and find one of the hippest bars in the world. The first thing you'll undoubtedly notice are the thousand or so maneki neko (lucky cat) statues. They preside over a room full of jazz and cinema regalia with posters, photos and album covers covering the walls. Film directors and critics stare out at you from the ultra-chic 1970s – the supposed era that taste forgot looking so damn good on the Japanese. Shelves are over-crammed with records that lean against each other. It's a decent-sized space for a music bar, so bring your friends along to indulge in well-priced drinks which go down easy with a relaxed, rather than pretentious, soundtrack of the ubiquitous jazz and soul. As with most listening bars there is a modest table charge which rises slightly after 9pm. You probably won't notice or care however, as the mood is right, the sounds chill and the chairs comfortable.

BAR MARTHA
バーマーサ

Ebisu

1-22-23 Ebisu, Shibuya-ku

Mon–Sun 7pm–3am

‣ Ebisu station, east exit

martha-records.com

In a small Ebisu backstreet enclave, you'll find a bar/listening library that prides itself on quality, spinning the deepest vintage vinyl soul cuts while serving up exceptional cocktails (mostly whisky) and gin and tonics. Music and vintage vibes are a serious business at Bar Martha, and they request that you tune in to their wavelength. This includes not taking photographs and not talking loudly – fair enough, this is a listening bar so listen. This is the true essence of a listening bar, slightly pretentious, dedicated to an impressive sound system (which reputedly cost around US$300,000) and neatly arranged and well looked after vinyl spinning on the turntable. Expect to be asked to wait in the 'airlock' for the song that is currently playing to finish before being let both in and out – if, like Steve, you kind of like the idea of that, then this is the place for you. Read the room: manners and dedication to the sounds will see that this bar hits the highest notes – just like Martha.

招
猫
明呪是無上呪是無等
能除一切苦眞實不虛
般若波羅蜜多呪即說呪曰
羯諦波羅羯諦波羅僧羯諦

MEGA DON QUIJOTE
メガドンキホーテ

Shibuya

28-6 Udagawacho, Shibuya-ku

Mon–Sun 24hr

‣ Shibuya station, exit A3a

donki.com

Donki, as it is affectionately known, is an out-of-control discount superstore and this MEGA Don Quijote store in Shibuya throbs with light and noise and never closes. A migraine waiting to happen, it's loud and over the top, a shopping theme park with a blue penguin for a mascot who points the way into an eight-floor retail maze of precariously balanced toys, comics, homewares, alcohol and dubious pharmaceuticals. It even has its own theme song, which insinuates itself into your head as you navigate the store. Impulse buyers won't know which way to turn. It is ultimately more trash than treasure, but food, gag gifts, sweets and electronic appliances are offset by luxury brands and a hard-to-beat selection of Asian beauty products at a price point for the people. Be careful where you walk: turn a corner from cleaning products and you could find yourself in an aisle full of sex toys and dubious manga costumes. Did we mention that it never closes? It's the perfect place for the somnambulant shopaholic in your life, especially when they desperately need those clip-on cat ears at 5am.

SPA LAQUA
スパラクーア

Bunkyo

1-1-1 Kasuga, Bunkyo-ku

Mon–Sun 11am–9am (the next day)

‣ Korakuen station, exit 5

laqua.jp

It may seem unusual to find a proper onsen (hot springs) that pumps water up from 1700m inside a water-world theme park that has a roller-coaster that sits, in part, on the roof of the onsen, but that's Tokyo. Once inside open-all-night Spa LaQua, you'll feel like you've been transported to a hot-springs resort. There are a variety of baths, including jet baths and baths of various temperatures, a milky white bath and a cold plunge bath, and some elaborate wash stations. If you are a sauna connoisseur you'll be in heaven, pay some extra yen for the Healing Baden where you'll find many saunas themed to different types of saunas from around the world. The large relaxation space allows you to kick back on couches, on reclining seats with TVs or in cosy booths while reading magazines, eating toasted sandwiches, pancakes or sundaes (for extra yen) all free of roller-coaster rumble (although you may experience the rumble of ambient snoring). You can pay an extra ¥2000 or so after 12am to stay over. It's a cheap and comfortable alternative to a capsule hotel. There is a ladies-only section and you can purchase eye masks and earplugs from the shop as well as fresh underclothes from a vending machine.

ONSEN NOTE

For other amazing all-night onsen (hot springs), visit Shinjuku's **Thermae-Yu** (Shinjuku-Sanchome station, exit E1) or **Edo-yu** (*see* p. 208).

LATE-NIGHT TEMPLES & SHRINES
夜の寺社巡り

Tokyo has some of Japan's most atmospheric shrines and temples, many of which have grounds that are open 24 hours. Shrine and temple buildings are often lit beautifully until around 11pm or 12am. While you will not be able to enter buildings, you can weave through the parklands and pathways with lamps, lanterns or just the moonlight to guide your way. It's atmospheric and moving and if you are a bit of an insomniac, the perfect way to spend some of those wide-awake hours.

Dating back to 628, **Senso-ji temple** (Asakusa station, exit 1) has grounds that are lit up until 11pm. The sight of the Kaminarimon gate and the five-storey pagoda illuminated is other-worldly. The 17th-century **Hanazono shrine** (Shinjuku-sanchome station, exit C5) contrasts the energy of the surrounding entertainment district with the deep tranquillity of the shrine, whose serene grounds are open 24 hours. If you're thinking of getting a bit loose in Kabukicho, head to the shrine, its torii gates and sacred trees enhanced by colourful lights, before heading to **Thermae-Yu** onsen. Hanazono also illuminates cherry blossom trees in spring. The gardens of **Nezu shrine** (Nezu station, exit 1) are open 24 hours and are renowned for historical wooden architecture and lush plantings. The illumination of the row of vermilion torii gates at night is spectacular. Add to the soft lighting of its thousands of azalea bushes during spring festivals and the shrine morphs into a spellbinding visual display. The **Kanda Myoujin shrine** (Ochanomizu station, Hijiri-bashi exit), has a dynamic red exterior and golden ornamentation, an arresting sight when the illuminations fall upon them as the sun sets. The grounds are open 24 hours, lit up until 11pm with an illumination display every Thursday night.

LIVE HOUSES
ライブハウス

Koenji is well known for its clutch of late-night live houses: underground dive bars and music-obsessed watering holes where bands sweat it out on small stages, giving their all for punters who enthusiastically swill booze and immerse themselves in the sounds. The eclectic blend of genres is a real education. Punk, electronica, punky electronica, jazz fusion, progressive metal, cute pop, cute pop metal — it's all on display and played with such a level of proficiency that you'll find yourself asking why the bands aren't on a world stadium tour. You never know quite what you're going to get, but you know it will be great or at the very least, memorable. Popular joints include **Koenji High**, **UFO Club**, **20,000V**, **Sound Studio Dom**, **Show Boat**, **Club Roots**, **Jirokichi** and **Muryoko Muzenji**. All of these live houses are within walking distance from Koenji station's main exit.

Other neighbourhoods well worth investigating for live houses include Shibuya, Shinjuku and the Edogawa area.

Toys, gaming, comics, characters, cartoons — when it comes to pop culture Tokyo is the world leader, running the gamut from lighthearted fun to super serious collecting and lifetime dedication. When we think back to many of our favourite pop characters or TV shows, they came straight out of Japan and mostly from Tokyo's NHK. These toys weren't just things to play with but icons that gladdened the heart and now bring waves of nostalgia to Japanese people and the many of us who grew up with them. Hello Kitty, Domo-Kun, Doraemon, Godzilla, Astro Boy, Gigantor, Ultraman, Sailor Moon and many more; they all made the leap to Western culture, highlighting the Japanese elevation of pop to cult status, something that plays out in megastores, art galleries, on clothes and in street art in Japan. So, if you've ever collected Pikachu swap cards, Sonny Angels or accidentally overfed your Tamagotchi, Tokyo is the city for you — a riot of colour and fun where pop culture is woven into the fabric of the city.

Pop culture also extends to books and music. From vinyl hunting to music megastores, Tokyo has everything music obsessives are looking for, and more. Don't even get us started on the plethora of book and magazine stores that, lucky for us, always have large English language sections. From the bookstores of Jimbocho, to the records stores of Shibuya and Shinjuku, Tokyo is a seemingly endless opportunity to uncover old favourites and discover new obsessions.

TOKYO

東京物語

POP

SHIBUYA PUBLISHING AND BOOKSELLERS
渋谷パブリッシング&ブックセラーズ

Tomigaya

17-3 Kamiyamacho, Shibuya-ku

Mon–Sun 11am–9pm

‣ Yoyogi-Koen station, exit 2

shibuyabooks.co.jp

The good folk at Shibuya Publishing and Booksellers have such fine-tuned taste that what starts out as a quick flick through the material on offer usually turns into an extended reading session. Shelves and trestle tables in this minimalist, relaxed store are stuffed with contemporary novels and magazines in Japanese and English. But that's only half the story. The bookstore also fosters and publishes local would-be writers. You'll find manga, novellas and tracts and rants of all kinds, lending the bookstore a seditious vibe, a very cool look in youthful, reactionary Tomigaya. Get wise: what you are casually scouring through could be the next big thing. There are regular publishing workshops and you can even rent out the in-store display box to peddle your zine or handmade stationery. Don't miss the store's merchandise, especially the tote bags, and spend time in the small nook of vintage novels, children's books and political tomes, often worth purchasing for the retro covers alone.

RHYTHM AND BOOKS
リズム&ブックス

Tomigaya

1-9-15 Tomigaya, Shibuya-ku

Wed–Fri 12–7pm, Sat–Mon 12–8pm

‣ Yoyogi-Koen station, exit 2

rhythm-books.com

Rhythm and Books is a tiny sliver of a store jammed from floor to ceiling with vintage books and, as the name suggests, music from Japan and Europe, all presided over by the dangling legs of a classic toy robot or perused by a retro-attired '80s model on the cover of a magazine. You'll have to crab-walk sideways to get through the skinny aisles, but the ramshackle collection of nostalgia is artfully chosen and you're sure to unearth some real treasures. The 'rhythm' part of the name is played out in a cache of second-hand CDs and vinyl that lean heavily towards jazz, pop and bossa nova, so no surprise there. The postcards with hilarious hairstyles from '70s pop stars are a treat, but eventually it's the wonderful children's books, vintage magazines, art exhibition fliers and novels with cool retro covers that make this place a joyful afternoon's browsing.

DESIGN NOTE

Look out for small exhibitions of local artists' work. The perfect indie take-home item to hang in your loungeroom.

BOOK LOVER'S NOTE

Don't miss the strangely extensive selection of books on kinoko (mushrooms), as Rhythm and Books seems to have an obsession with them.

DESIGN BOOK NOTE

Book and Sons (Gakugeidaigaku station, east exit) curate an exquisite selection of design and typography tomes.

DESIGN NOTE

The exterior of the Daikanyama T-Site building features monolithic white boxes that are made up of a repeated pattern of the letter T, designed by Klein Dytham Architecture.

COW BOOKS
カウブックス

Nakameguro

1-14-11 Aobadai, Meguro-ku

Tues–Sun 1–9pm

› Nakameguro station, west exit

cowbooks.stores.jp

The staff at Cow Books love their tomes so much they actually take them on daytrips back to the forest 'where they came from', to give them a sense of belonging. Seriously. This left-of-centre bookstore specialises in out-of-print books, mostly from the '50s and '60s and the underground press. The selection will take you on a journey through social politics, the Beat Generation, the hippy subculture of San Francisco's Haight-Ashbury, Black Power, art theory, music and poetry. If you feel the need to start a revolution or new social movement (while kicking back with one of their excellent coffees), you'll find a book or leaflet here to show you how. Counterculture icons like Timothy Leary and William S. Burroughs lead the way, but you'll also stumble across some first editions by lesser-known modern authors and some seriously sought-after art books. Not a lot of books about cows, however, so don't go in there expecting to expand your knowledge of agriculture.

DAIKANYAMA T-SITE
代官山 T-SITE

Daikanyama

17-5 Sarugakucho, Shibuya-ku

Mon–Sun 7am–11pm

› Daikanyama station, central exit

store.tsite.jp/daikanyama

This biosphere dedicated to all things peruse-worthy has become a magnet for bibliophiles and weekend browsers alike. Not just an extremely impressive architectural hub – although the breezeblock and glass mega-space is worth the visit alone – T-Site has an absurdly extensive range of books of every genre, including a large selection of English releases (we were excessively proud to see our own books on the shelves of the travel section). One of the main drawcards is 'magazine street' which boasts around 30,000 vintage magazines, mostly from the '60s and '70s, as well as the latest publications. Design book lovers are spoilt for choice here, as are anime lovers who have their own zone. A dedicated stationery area has a range of fountain pens and paper products to delight those who still like to send off snail mail. Awesome workstations and reading sections turn the landmark building into a mini library and public study. On the 2nd floor you can leaf through a book or two at the cafe, **Anjin**. On the grounds you'll also find an unmissable gallery space, **BorneLund Toyshop**, convenience store **Famima**, **Green Dog** grooming salon and **Ivy Place**, a hugely popular cafe and bar. You could easily lose a day in this mega-complex, and on Sundays, hordes of Tokyo-ites do just that.

MUSIC NOTE

Also check out Koenji's **Record Boy** and **Uptown Record Store**.

DESIGN NOTE

Jet Set has its own excellent merch, and also sells cassette tapes and record cloths. Why not check out the sartorial style of the staff for inspo on your next gig outfit?

BE-IN RECORD
ビー・インレコーズ

Koenji

2F, 3-57-8 Koenji-Minami, Suginami-ku

Mon–Sun 12.30–8.30pm

‣ Koenji station, south exit

bein.co.jp

Be-In Record is a treasure trove of collectible vinyl and a haven for the obsessive fan of first releases and test pressings. Music aficionados will have a minor meltdown as they madly rifle through the amazing collection (Beatles and Stones fans, in particular will be in seventh heaven). When they finally raise their heads, hours will have past and bored partners will be long gone. Boxes crammed with records take up most of the room: there's barely space to squeeze between them. Most genres are covered, including rock, pop, punk, R&B, soul, jazz and heavy metal; 1960's psych, garage and freakbeat is a specialty, and there is plenty of indie as well in the expertly sourced selection. Prices for the rarer records can definitely be on the steep side, but serious collectors won't mind paying for that much-sought-after Northern soul gem. For music buffs on a budget, you'll be happy to know that there are also some affordable finds.

JET SET
ジェットセット

Shimokitazawa

2-33-12 Kitazawa, Setagaya-ku

Mon–Sun 12–8pm

‣ Shimokitazawa station, east exit

jetsetrecords.net

Hidden away in a non-descript building, Jet Set record store is a mecca for house and techno DJs, as well as a regular shopping haunt for anyone obsessed with independent music. The collection is crammed into every nook and cranny, only leaving room for a listening station with a couple of turntables where you can try before you buy. The name hints at the overall décor, with trinkets and figurines from the swinging '60s and '70s and emblems of world travel dotted about the space, inspiring you to hop onto a Learjet and dream of all the record stores you'll visit in various countries around the world while sipping on a martini. For the claustrophobic, there's a very comprehensive online store, but you might prefer not to miss the atmosphere here, which harks back to the good old days of hunting through a favourite store for the latest vinyl (or CD) releases. So have a scout around, as you're sure to find something interesting, challenging or even life-changing amongst the impressive selection.

BIG LOVE RECORDS
ビッグ・ラブ・レコーズ

Harajuku

3F, 2-31-3 Jingumae, Shibuya-ku

Mon 3–8pm, Tues–Sun 1–10pm

› Meiji-Jingumae station, exit 5

bigloverecords.jp

Ever the urban explorer, you'll have to venture to the edge of Harajuku and down a random side street, then up several flights of stairs to find BIG LOVE RECORDS. It's worth it though, as this is one of the most respected indie record store/bar/cafes in Tokyo, nay, the world! It's amazing what they pack into a tiny frame here, with racks of vinyl, CDs and tapes with an indie/alternative leaning squeezed between a bar that looks like a Mexican cantina and a tiny rustic cafe that makes an excellent brew. The zines, along with the various musical formats for sale, will transport you to the glory days of the 1980s and '90s, when music could be held and admired, and owned, rather than rented. It's not all natsukashii (happy nostalgia) though – they only deal in new import indie releases here. The independent ethos extends to the bar's rotating crop of rare Japanese craft beers, which you can taste test while listening to some truly select tunes. For those missing the BIG LOVE ethos when they leave Japan, there is also an excellent online record store.

CITY COUNTRY CITY
シティーカントリーシティー

Shimokitazawa

2-12-13 Kitazawa, Setagaya-ku

Thurs–Mon 12–10pm

› Shimokitazawa station, central exit

Seek out the tiny street sign and take the wobbly lift up four floors to emerge into this pocket-sized vintage vinyl store and cafe. Owner Keiichi Sokabe was the lead singer of Japanese cult '90s indie band Sunny Day Service, and his love of music shines through in the selection of pre-loved world music, disco, indie rock, house and space funk records that populate the racks. Photos of DJs and band autographs on the wall hint that there are good finds here and Sokabe makes regular international trips to forage for quality records. In the cafe, sip a latte or cold beer while enjoying the tunes, or order a simple pasta or curry (very inexpensive with coffee, tea or juice included). After dark, City Country City morphs into a listening bar where you can immerse yourself in the sounds of Sokabe's latest obsessions.

MUSIC MEGASTORES
大型ミュージックストア

Tokyo's mega-music hubs may not be small and independently owned, but they have collections of music, new and old and in many formats that truly boggle the mind. **Disc Union** (Shinjuku station, east central exit) has a plethora of stores in Shinjuku (and a choice store in Shibuya) where a day may not be enough for the music enthusiast. If you can't find what you want in these stores, you must have the most obscure taste in the world. Watch people flick through racks of records before getting misty-eyed and gleefully grabbing that long-sought-after pop or rock holy grail. The test pressings lining the walls of most stores will make your jaw drop, both for the rarity and the price. One-time American brand **Tower Records** (Shibuya station, exit A7a) is now a nostalgic dream in the USA, closed forever in 1979, but don't despair as Tower was brought back to life in Tokyo in 2002. Although music went decidedly online and record stores went decidedly offline, Tower survived the vicissitudes by sheer determination and by having seven floors of music, books and paraphernalia, stocked to the brim and up-to-the-minute, perfectly placed in busy Shibuya. The building is iconic now, a retro-futurist space rocket with yellow-piped trim and a body of what looks like grey LEGO bricks. Also resuscitated in Shibuya is **HMV** (Shibuya station, exit A2), having tragically collapsed in the UK, leaving only pleasant memories of vinyl searching behind. The expansive store has a particularly tasty section that deals in vintage records and pre-loved cassettes, DVDs and more. Neatly arranged and easily navigated, the store blends both rare and expensive finds with cheaper purchases and really excels in the independent and alternative genres. Steve has spent many a happy afternoon here and even stumbled upon a few unexpected finds. Get tactile. It's so much better than shopping online, isn't it?

ANIME, MANGA AND COLLECTIBLES
アニメ・マンガ・コレクターズグッズ

'They're not toys, they're collectibles.' Never has this been truer than in Tokyo, and especially in the otaku (obsessive collector) epicentre area of Akihabara, where you'll find endless stores dedicated to anime, manga, models, vintage gaming, figurines and more.

Mandarake (Akihabara station, Electric Town exit) has major stores in Akihabara and Shibuya (although the head store is in Nakano). Starting in 1987 as a second-hand comic store, Mandarake expanded to include an eye-popping range of pre-loved toys, anime, manga and all manner of vintage collectibles filling floor-to-ceiling shelves in multi-floored buildings. You'll find what you are looking for here, and as time goes on, Mandarake almost becomes a museum of the history of Japanese pop-culture curiosities. **Super Potato** (Akihabara station, Electric Town exit) on the other hand, deals in vintage video games and consoles. In the Akihabara store, several floors are stuffed with refurbished Nintendo 64 and Xbox. Pacman your way through the store, bleeps and bloops emanating from every corner, drawing energy from the electronic entertainment of your youth (or your parents' youth). Don't be surprised if you suddenly find that you've become pixelated while in-store. Games of the past now live to be played another day. Check out the top floor, a video games parlour that is complete with working machines and retro snacks.

COLLECTOR'S NOTE

If you're into collecting the Blythe doll, **Junie Moon** in Daikanyama (Daikanyama station, central exit) is a mecca for the doll's army of fans and serves as a catwalk for her to rock her latest styles.

FOODIE NOTE

Shiro-Hige's **Cream Puff Factory** (Kichijoji station, south exit or Setagaya-daichi station) is close by and makes delicious sweet treats in the shape of Totoro. They also have a limited-edition 'raisins butter sand' Catbus biscuit. It is owned by Miyazaki's sister-in-law.

GHIBLI MUSEUM
三鷹の森ジブリ
美術館

Mitaka

1-1-83 Shimorenjaku, Mitaka-shi

Wed–Mon 10am–6pm

‣ Mitaka station, south exit

ghibli-museum.jp

Anime fans make what can only be described as a religious pilgrimage out to Mitaka to visit the Ghibli Museum. Opened in 2001, and designed by master animator and head of Studio Ghibli Hayao Miyazaki himself, the museum offers an immersive experience into an enigmatic world. The museum's whimsical design reflects the studio's films, and exhibitions breathe life into celebrated characters and scenes, from beloved movies like *Spirited Away*, *My Neighbor Totoro*, and *Princess Mononoke*. Our favourite feature is a special exhibition area that rotates regularly, focusing on different aspects of animation and the studio's creative process as well as a behind-the-scenes look at the animation process. One of the museum's popular exhibits is the super-soft life-sized Catbus from *My Neighbor Totoro*, which children can board and pretend they are on a magical journey. The museum also has a cosy theatre that screens exclusive short films made by Studio Ghibli. The lush surrounding grounds add to the museum's enchantment, a tranquil setting presided over by a 5m-high robot soldier from *Castle in the Sky*. All tickets must be bought in advance online, and then picked up from Lawson convenience stores.

Travel can be expensive, so this chapter is for the budget conscious who don't want to compromise on amazing experiences. Whether you are a history buff, into art, walks in nature, or enjoy staring in awe at some of the world's most astounding views, there are plenty of opportunities in Tokyo to experience Japanese culture and ingenuity without unlocking your wallet and letting the moths out.

Iconic Tokyo destinations like Hachiko Square and nearby Shibuya Scramble cost nothing to enjoy. It's free to explore elegant shopping centres, famous streets, towering neon jungles, notable temples and shrines, and admire the city's astounding architecture.

There are some spectacular traditional Japanese gardens with long histories that charge an entry fee, however you can chill out with the locals in the city's free parks and gardens.

If you want to see some memorable Tokyo moments without unfurling your rolls of yen, check out our recommended Tokyo spaces and places that you won't believe you can experience for free. There are even toilets designed by leading architects and industrial designers that cost nothing to use.

TOKYO

FREE ZONE

東京物語

THE TOKYO TOILET PROJECT
渋谷 東京トイレプロジェクト

Wim Wenders' moving film *Perfect Days* (2023) chronicled small pockets of beauty in the protagonist Hirayama's daily life. Our hero also cleans toilets for a living. As with many things in Japan, these are not just toilets but community-led projects designed to enhance one's day. Due to the popularity of this touching film, a pilgrimage of sorts has led cinema buffs and design enthusiasts to make their own perfect day excursion — to toilets!

In the sprawling ward of Shibuya, The Tokyo Toilet Project has commissioned a range of public toilets created by architects and designers, to be used by anyone regardless of gender. High-profile names like Marc Newson, Kengo Kuma, Tadao Ando and Toyo Ito were given free rein to experiment. Flush with ideas, they plunged into the project, and not content to sit on their success, they made a splash (sorry). The designs have no uniformity, linked only by their striking exteriors and contemporary fixtures. There are colourful bunkers, mushroom-like domes, circular pods, illuminated boxes, a wooden plank maze and a clear-glass toilet that turns opaque when the door is locked (there were a few problems when this malfunctioned in mid 2024).

All of the toilets have been built in the Shibuya ward, a broad area taking in Shibuya, Harajuku, Omotesando, Yoyogi, Ebisu, Sendagaya and more. Look for the constructions in Ebisu at **Ebisu station west exit**, **Ebisu park** and **Ebisu East park**. Marc Newson's toilet can be found at **Urasando** in Sendagaya, and Kengo Kuma's in **Nabeshima Shoto park**. Toyo Ito's pods are located at **Yoyogi Hachiman station** and other toilets can be found at **Higashi Sanchome station** and **Hiroo East park**. If you feel the need, why not try them all?

MEIJI-JINGU SHRINE
明治神宮

Yoyogi

1-1 Yoyogikamizonocho, Shibuya-ku

Mon–Sun sunrise to sunset

‣ Harajuku station, west exit

meijijingu.or.jp

The contrast between the city and the serene, whispering glades of the Meiji Shinto shrine couldn't be more acute. Head out of Harajuku station and turn towards the towering Ichino torii gate. Once through you'll find yourself in woods with small torii gates, rows of blessed sake barrels (for the gods), statues and bridges. On a sunny day the light here is mystical, filtered gently through the tall cedars. The path, known as the 'Shrine Forest' is dense with chinquapin, oak and camphor trees, amongst its 350 varieties, all planted as an 'eternal forest' constantly rejuvenating itself. You are well out of the madness of the city now. The shrine itself is a relic of old Tokyo. When Emperor Meiji died in 1912, he was deified at this shrine (although he wasn't interred here). The original shrine was rebuilt after World War II, and now stands proud and impressive, ageing gracefully amongst the thick forest. It is our hope that when you are there you will get to see a truly beautiful Shinto wedding ceremony, which are often held on the grounds of the shrine. The forest (with its 120,000 trees) and shrine grounds are free, but it's worth paying to enter the newly built **Meiji Jingu Museum**, designed by Kengo Kuma.

GOTOKU-JI TEMPLE
豪徳寺

Setagaya

2-24-7 Gotokuji, Setagaya-ku

Mon–Sun 6am–5pm

‣ Miyanosaka station

gotokuji.jp

A brief 'paws' on anyone's cat-inerary, Gotoku-ji temple houses a small shrine 'Shofukuden' famous as the birthplace of the maneki neko, or lucky cat. On this very spot a feudal lord was saved from lightning by a cat who beckoned him to shelter. The shrine is populated by a clowder of cat statues en masse, arranged in tiers in all shapes and sizes. Don't miss Sanju-no-to pagoda where you can look for cats carved into the woodwork amongst other animals from the Chinese zodiac. You can catch the 'cat tram' from Shimotakaido station to Gotoku-ji temple; neko enthusiasts will think it's the cat's pyjamas when the cat-shaped tram, called Kofuku-no-Manekineko Densha, trundles around the corner. It's about both the journey and the destination with the tram's kawaii (cute) interior of paw print floors and cat handles. While not on the tourist trail, Gotoku-ji temple is loved by feline fans, so arrive early for photos. Don't forget to buy a small lucky cat for your desk at home. Purrfect!

CULTURE NOTE

Senso-ji temple in Asakusa is an exceptional temple that won't cost you a penny to enter. The street food stalls on the walk up to the temple may 'eat' into your budget however.

TRAVELLER'S NOTE

Miyanosaka station is the closest stop (5min walk) to Gotoku-ji temple. It's on the Setagaya line, which runs irregularly. Setagaya and Sangenjaya are two areas with a local feel and good food and art that we love to visit on this neighbourhood line, too.

GGG GINZA GRAPHIC GALLERY
ギンザ・グラフィック・ギャラリー

Ginza

DNP Ginza Building B1F, 7-7-2 Ginza, Chuo-ku
Wed–Sat 11am–7pm
‣ Ginza station, exit A2
dnpfcp.jp

On most trips to Tokyo, we'll visit the Ginza Graphic Gallery (stylised as ggg) to find out what's happening in the world of graphic design and advertising. Hiding in plain sight in busy central Ginza, you'll find the gallery in the DNP building. Specialising in all manner of graphics, both cutting edge and retro over two floors, we always discover updates in technology, logo creation and just a hint of the avant-garde to remind you that art and fashion filter both into and out of trends in graphic design. There is always something to surprise and inspire in the themed exhibitions which feature the work of well-known and established artists and graphic designers. The evolution of design is represented with each expertly curated exhibition – and it's easy to see how the roots of Japanese handcrafts – from calligraphy to kimono prints and ceramics, have influenced what is today some of the best graphic design in the world. A broad range of mediums represented include video, posters, packaging, painting, screen print and design models. And entry is free, although you can buy the exhibition booklet as a keepsake or head next door to **MMM** to look through the range of books from prior exhibitions.

FREE CITY VIEWS
無料のシティビュー

There are many towering buildings in Tokyo's cluttered skyscape, so it's no surprise that there are plenty of spots where you can pay for a premium view of the expansive cosmopolis. Before you break your self-imposed daily allowance however, take advantage of these amazing free vistas, where your credit card remains unscathed, and vertigo is your only concern.

The **Caretta Shiodome** building (Shiodome station, exit 5 or 6), also home to the Ad Museum (*see* p. 186), features a free 'sky view' from the 46th floor, 200m high and takes in the spectacular sights of the bay area, Odaiba and the Rainbow Bridge below. **Tokyo Solamachi** (Oshiage station exit A2 or B3) has views from the 30th floor that take in the monumental Skytree, giving you a chance to view the impressive tower, famous for its own views. The **Tokyo Metropolitan Government Building** (Tochomae station, exit A4) has long been a place for Tokyo-ites to go to get a free peek at the city's vast scope. On a clear day you can even catch a glimpse of Mount Fuji from the 45th floor observatory, as well as a panoramic sweep of the city that takes in the Skytree and Tokyo Tower. **Yebisu Sky Garden Place** (Ebisu station, east exit, then take Yebisu Sky Walk) has two observation decks on the 38th and 39th floors and views of Fuji ... again, on a clear day. The 25th floor of **Bunkyo Civic Center Observation Lounge** (Korakuen station, exit 5) has a 330-degree panoramic view of Tokyo that includes the Skytree and Mount Fuji. Also try Sangenjaya's **Carrot Tower** (Sangenjaya station, east exit).

THE HARUKI MURAKAMI LIBRARY
村上春樹ライブラリー

Waseda

Waseda University, east gate

1-6-4 Nishiwaseda, Shinjuku-ku

Thurs–Tues 10am–5pm

3204 4614

‣ Waseda station, exits 2 or 3B

The Waseda International House of Literature (The Haruki Murakami Library), designed by Kengo Kuma, is an angular white block augmented by a curve of sculptural metal. The chapel-like exterior is appropriate, as this is a religious pilgrimage to Waseda University, famed writer Murakami's alma mater. On entering, an intricate wooden slat archway continues the religious theme and houses the majority of works from Murakami's book collection, some 3000 tomes that feature first editions and rarities. Study rooms, reading spaces, cosy pods and communal tables give the space a contemplative air. The quiet, reflective space also features a free gallery showing works from artists with a like-minded aesthetic to Murakami. A mid-century-styled reading lounge and listening space features cosy couches where you can enjoy a playlist of jazz and classical works. The records played are displayed on the walls, the same vinyl spun in Murakami's pre-novelist business venture, the jazz cafe Peter Cat, that he started with his wife Yoko Takahashi in 1974. Records from Herbie Mann, Masahiko Sato and 'Sentimental Mood' by Barbara Carroll sit alongside Beethoven's 9th symphony. The many books on display provide inspiration for you to sit quietly and perhaps pen your own bestseller. This is a shrine to creativity and cool that commands respect and demands reverential silence.

INTELLECTUAL NOTE

Waseda University was founded in 1882 by Samurai scholar Okuma Shigenobu, who would become Japan's 5th prime minister. It has an odd mix of buildings reflecting a blend of Japanese and Western culture. Don't miss the beautiful **Okuma Garden**, a chisen kaiyu (strolling pond) garden that was once the grounds of Shigenobu's family mansion.

GALLERIES & MUSEUMS
無料のギャラリーと美術館

Tokyo's commitment to making art and culture accessible to all is played out in a wonderful array of free museums and galleries. In KITTE (*see* p. 34), you'll find **Intermediatheque** (Tokyo Station, Marunouchi south exit), an atmospheric museum that hosts the science, culture and heritage collections of Tokyo University. The museum, over two floors, has some impressive displays including giant spider crabs, whale bones, a range of taxidermy, an Egyptian mummy and objects from the world of geography, the arts, geology and mathematics. In the basement of the Caretta Shiodome building, you'll find **ADMT**, known as the Ad Museum (Shimbashi station, Shiodome exit), an extensive free exhibition of advertising and graphics from as far back as the Edo period (1603—1867), with a fun rotation of retro ads from the '60s to '90s. **The Meguro Parasitological Museum** (Meguro station, west exit) has the gross-out factor that makes it fun for kids but those with a scientific mind will be astounded at the startling parasite facts. The exhibition includes a 9m tape worm found in an unlucky human host and various icky specimens appearing in bottles and cases, and later in your nightmares. **Ikebukuro Bosaikan** (Ikeburo station, Metropolitan exit) is a museum that addresses disaster prevention. Standout points are a shaking room that simulates an earthquake, a smoke maze, and a place where you can actually live out your ultimate fantasy and let off a fire extinguisher.

Other free museums are **Mitaka Picture Book House** (Mitaka station, south exit) and **Anime Tokyo Station** (Ikebukuro station, east exit).

FREE GREEN SPACES
無料の緑の場所

Tokyo may be a tangle of concrete and steel, skyscrapers piercing holes in the cloudy skies and megalithic department stores crowding the skyline, but the city's expansive gardens, parks and forests offer the chance to stroll, picnic and breathe. **Ueno park** (*see* p. 67) is a vast area that hosts many memorable museums and some excellent shrines and temples. Plantings include the famous lotus flowers on the lake, spectacular when in bloom in July and August, sakura (cherry blossoms) that swathe the pond in pink in April during hanami (cherry blossom season), plum trees, ginko and maple, peonies, chrysanthemum and azaleas. **Chidorigafuchi park** (Kudanshita station, exit 2) along the moat of the Imperial Palace Gardens features spectacular cherry blossoms in season, night illuminations and lush greenery. **Hibiya park** (Kasumigaseki station, exit B2, or Hibiya station, exit A10 or A14) is Tokyo's first modern, Western-style green space and features cherry blossoms, tulips, hydrangeas, azaleas and lilies. **Inokashira park** (Inokashira station, park exit) is a delightful escape on the Inokashira line from Shibuya. A gift from the Emperor Taisho in 1917, the park is based around a large central pond where you can float on swan-shaped paddle boats, with excellent views of the blossoms during hanami. With over 11,000 trees including sakura, red pine and cypresses, and nearly 13,000 shrubs, most notably azaleas, the park is spectacular in all seasons. The popular **Ghibli Museum** (*see* p. 175) can be found in the south-west section of the park.

TRAVELLER'S NOTE

Don't miss **Yoyogi park**, an expansive stretch of greenery which is excellent for cycling (Harajuku station, exit 2, or access from Meiji-Jingumae, Yoyogi-koen or Yoyogi-hachiman stations).

Edo was the original name for Tokyo and encapsulates a period from 1603 to 1868, an extended historical era which saw a thriving port town blossom into the beginning stages of the vast metropolis of Tokyo that we know today. Also known as the Tokugawa period, and presided over by the Tokugawa shogunate, and the daimyo, or feudal lords, the Edo period was characterised by stability, peace and a flourishing of art, craft and culture that all citizens could enjoy.

Edo period arts and crafts that are still revered today include ukiyo-e (woodblock printmaking), nanga (Japanese painting) and kabuki theatre. Economical and inventive use of indigo-dyed textiles led to creativity in pattern and print and the sustainable practice of boro (repairing something tatted) with sashiko (repetitive stitching). It was also a time when handmade utilitarian items were beautified by artisans to enhance everyday living.

Unearthing the remnants of Edo in Tokyo will find you stepping back in time into traditional paper stores, art museums, onsen (hot springs), shrines, samurai strongholds and sumo stables, and even an historic cemetery. You can take your time-travelling a step further and eat at Japan's first bakery or try the stew that sumos eat at a Chanko Nabe restaurant.

There are also otherworldly green spaces that were grown and sculpted in the Edo period — traditional and historic strolling gardens that were once the domain of the upper classes, but now you can immerse yourself in nature and forget you're surrounded by a metropolis, while gaining insight into the flora and fauna of the city, both now and in Edo times.

So why not take on Tokyo like a samurai, eat like a sumo, and have a holiday with all the drama of a kabuki show?

東京物語

TOKYO

EDO

HISTORY NOTE

Haibara's online museum on its website is a wonderful insight into its world of paper.

OMIYAGE NOTE

A range of stationery, paper mobiles, greeting cards and good-luck charms are perfect for souvenirs.

HAIBARA
榛原

Nihonbashi

2-7-1 Nihonbashi, Chuo-ku
Mon–Fri 10am–6.30pm, Sat–Sun 10am–5.30pm
‣ Nihonbashi station, exit B6
haibara.co.jp

Set amongst Nihonbashi's looming, grey skyscrapers and department stores you'll find a small, elegant paper shop, founded in 1806 towards the end of the Edo period (1603–1867). Haibara's architecture literally comes gift wrapped, a modernist black box with the Haibara logo appearing on the front as a red wax seal. The building speaks of the future, but is softened by a tiled canopy and noren (traditional fabric curtains), a nod to the past. Stepping inside is like entering a world where you can shop like you are in old Edo. Floor-to-ceiling displays showcase beautiful paper and original woodblock prints from 200 years of classic washi paper design. Searching through the drawers of paper and envelopes of various shapes and sizes uncovers bold and intricately designed chiyogami (silk screen prints), pattern boxes and fans that make perfect presents. Their classic 'letter paper,' with simple lines and a thin stripe of colour around the edges, has been a favourite of many famous writers over the years. So head into Haibara for inspiration – it's time to think inside the box.

ISETATSU
いせ辰

Yanaka

2-18-9 Yanaka, Taito-ku
Mon–Sun 10am–6pm
‣ Sendagi station, exit 1
isetatsu.com

Established in 1864, Isetatsu is still owned and run by the founding family, now in its fifth generation. The store's extensive array of beautifully printed and patterned paper use traditional methods to make Edo chiyogami (colourful woodblock printed paper). The themes and patterns usually relate to nature, brightly coloured flowers, leaves, seasons and fanciful tableaux of animals doing people things. Kept in large wooden drawers which can be extended out so you can fully appreciate the scale of the designs, these are works of art, so intricate and beautiful are the patterns. One of the uses for Chiyogami was for the amusement of children which is translated onto fans and toys about the store to delight young ones. On a visit many years ago, we bought two sheets of exquisite paper. They hang on our wall to this day, adding a chapter to the rich tapestry of our Japan adventures.

SEARCHING FOR EDO
江戸を歩く

In these areas you'll find whispers of old Edo. Many shops are run by the descendants of the original families, sometimes going back up to ten generations, with skills passed down through the ages and proudly carrying on the traditions of their ancestors. You can find these artisan stores especially around the Shitemachi area (the worker's area in the Edo period), which includes Taito, Sumida and Chuo wards. The Yamanote areas (samurai and notable people) include Shibuya, Shinjuku and Meguro wards, however these areas were decimated in both the Great Kanto earthquake in 1923 and bombing during World War II, wiping out history and reinventing the city as a modern metropolis. Asakusa, Ueno and the Yanesen area (Yanaka, Nezu and Sendagi) are some of the best places to find remnants and experiences in Tokyo that can instantly transport you back to the Edo period. They give you a glimpse into the evolution of the city, the atmosphere of simpler times and, due to the country's isolationism, the very stark differences between the East and the West of the pre-modern era.

SHIROKIYA NAKAMURA DENBEI
白木屋伝兵衛

Kyobashi

3-9-8 Kyobashi, Chuo-ku
Mon–Sun 10am–7pm
‣ Kyobashi station, exit 1

'Tools for life' is a saying you'll hear a lot in Japan. Utilitarian items that make daily tasks enjoyable and good quality items that do not break or wear out and can be repaired and fixed. So, when we come home from a Tokyo trip and tell friends we bought a new broom or dustpan, we may receive a perplexing look which changes to understanding when they see the desirable elegance of the materials' construction and design. Shirokiya Nakamura Denbei feels like a shop out of time. Whenever we step into the unassuming store, we get a nostalgic sense of the craftmanship of times gone by and yet it is so very relevant to today's eco-conscious society. Founded in 1830 and now presided over by the eighth-generation owner Satoru Nakamura, the store is famous for their traditional cleaning tools. The 'Edo-style' brooms are high quality and made from natural materials like bamboo and sorghum, ideal for sweeping tatami mats, carpets, and hard floors. The Harimi dustpans, crafted with persimmon tannin, are excellent, stylish additions to your home. Handmade by artisans using traditional Japanese techniques, their products emphasise sustainability and eco-friendly practices. They're biodegradable and of course require no electricity to use, making them the perfect, progressive purchase that also gives your home a wistful hint of history.

SUMO CULTURE AND CHANKO NABE RESTAURANTS
両国で相撲

Ryogoku

Referenced in books as far back as 712, but becoming a professional sport in the Edo period, Sumo (rikishi) wrestling is deeply intertwined with the way of the samurai. Sumo wrestling is a uniquely Japanese sport with a complex array of tactical manoeuvres and a startling display of strength all presided over by a rigid dedication to tradition, spirituality and sumo culture. As the centre of sumo, Ryogoku is an Edo period 'shitemachi' hotspot, a historical slice of old Tokyo, rich in sumo culture, that features sumo training stables, a museum, restaurants and **Ryogoku Kokugikan Arena**, where most of Japan's sumo wrestling matches are held today. The sumo museum is inside the arena, where you can get a glimpse into the lives and history of sumo, or if you like you can visit the sumo stables and see young sumo in training.

The precinct's **Chanko Nabe restaurants** serve the hearty stew that is essential to a rikishi's diet. With a convivial atmosphere and often run by retired sumo, Chanko Nabe joints are rowdy affairs where the over-stuffed hot-pot can challenge the most capacious stomach. Hot-pots usually include fish, tofu and vegetables bolstered by a protein in the form of a meatball or seafood ball. We recommend ordering one between two, but you can set your own limits according to self-belief. **Kawasaki Chanko** is considered the first Chanko Nabe restaurant, opened in 1937 by a renowned sumo of the era, and it's well worth a visit for some Edo period authenticity.

KIMURAYA
木村屋

Ginza

4-5-7 Ginza, Chuo-ku
Mon–Sun 10am–8pm
‣ Ginza station, exit A9
ginzakimuraya.jp

What does samurai Kimura Kenjiro do when the Edo period comes to an end, and he needs to make dough? Swap his sword for a kitchen knife and apply his knowledge and dedication to a new profession. His namesake bakery was founded in 1869, merging tradition and skill with the dedication of a samurai. Long considered Japan's first bakery, the main store stands proudly on Ginza's Chuo-dori. Popular now, as it has been for over 150 years, at 10am, just before they open, a polite queue will start to form. Staff will be ready to take orders of sakadane (rice sourdough) and sakekasu anpan (fermented sake lees) , and the soft bread is then filled with adzuki bean, butter bean, fig or cream cheese. Seasonal varieties will fill the shelves, such as sour pickled cherry blossoms in spring. Another standout buy is the baguette with butter and adzuki bean, or their exceptional shokupan which comes in a big fluffy loaf. Stock up on Kimuraya pastries, which are perfect for picnics in nearby Hibiya park or the Imperial Palace Gardens.

FOODIE NOTE
The 2nd floor cafe makes a delicious morning or lunch set.

KIYOSUMI TEIEN
清澄庭園

Kiyosumi-shirakawa

3-3-9 Kiyosumi, Koto-ku

Mon–Sun 9am–5pm

‣ Kiyosumi-Shirakawa station, exit A3

tokyo-park.or.jp/park/kiyosumi

Located in a peaceful area known for coffee and one of Tokyo's best galleries, **MOT** (*see* p. 69), is Kiyosumi Teien garden – a serene escape we always make time to visit. Owned by a feudal lord during the Edo period (1603–1867), the garden was transformed in the Meiji period (1868–1912) by the Iwasaki family, founders of Mitsubishi. In 1932 it was donated to the city, allowing the public to enjoy its unique beauty. A Kaiyu-style (circuit) garden, it inspires a leisurely walk around the expansive Dai-sensui pond, over rocks and bridges and past wondrous foliage. Unique stones, carefully collected by the Iwasaki family, feature prominently throughout, blending seamlessly with the pond and waterways. The gentle murmur of the city provides a soft backdrop to the tranquil environment, where tortured pine trees twist poetically towards the water, protected by yukitsuri ropes. Rest at the Ryo-tei floating teahouse (reservations required) for wagashi (Japanese sweets) and matcha while watching turtles, koi and wistful herons. One of the garden's highlights is the famous haiku by Basho, 'The Sound of a Frog Jumping into an Old Pond,' carved into a rock. The garden's thoughtful planting offers beauty across all seasons, from cherry blossoms in spring to the golden and auburn hues of autumn. Elegant bentos are available to pre-order online up to a week in advance so why not plan a picnic?

SEASONAL NOTE

While we love visiting this garden year-round, our favourite time is early June when the rainy season's clouds soften the light, casting magical shadows on the pine needles, moss and lichen.

RIKUGIEN
六義園

Komagome

6-16-3 Honkomagome, Bunkyo-ku

Mon–Sun 9am–5pm

‣ Komagome station, south exit

tokyo-park.or.jp/park/rikugien

A prime example of Edo period (1603–1867) landscape design, Rikugien garden is one of our favourite retreats from the city and can be found in easily accessible Komagome in Bunkyo ward. Built for the 5th Tokugawa shogun, it was completed in 1702 and opened to the public in 1938. You can see why a stressed shogun would need such a space to stroll around in and, happily, we can enjoy it today to achieve the same sense of tranquillity. This elegant garden can be explored within an hour. It stretches around a serene lake with a central island, providing a captivating setting to admire vibrant autumn maple leaves or the soft pink of sakura (cherry blossoms) in spring, both beautifully illuminated at night. Bridges cross tranquil lakes, meandering streams weave around twisted trees, and a climb to the highest hill offers a stunning panoramic view of the garden's many features. The garden's name, 'Garden of the Six Principles', refers to six elements of Chinese-influenced Waka poetry, which served as the inspiration for its 88 distinct sections, small re-creations of scenes described in the poems, each marked by a stone (only 32 of these stone markers remain today).

CULTURE NOTE

Enjoy a bowl of matcha at **Fukiagejaya Tea House**, the perfect setting within the gardens to contemplate nature.

THE SUMIDA HOKUSAI MUSEUM
すみだ北斎美術館

Sumida

2-7-2 Kamezawa, Sumida-ku

Tues–Sun 9.30am–5.30pm

‣ Ryogoku station, exit A5

hokusai-museum.jp

This strikingly contemporary museum in Sumida ward is a tribute to the artist Katsushika Hokusai, best known for one of the world's most iconic works of art, *The Great Wave Off Kanagawa*. Known to westerners as *The Hokusai Wave*, the ukiyo-e woodblock print was made in 1829–32 in the later Edo period. Hokusai's influence on Western art, particularly on Van Gogh and the Impressionists was immeasurable. The museum, designed by Sejima Kazuyo of SANAA architects, is possibly a glinting, metallic abstraction of the wave, a sci-fi futurist block that has no bad angles, making it a photographer's dream to frame. Inside, a permanent exhibition of the master's work is showcased in bold and artistic ways, and there is also a space for transitory exhibits. One of the original woodblock prints of the classic wave resides here, amongst the many iconic Hokusai works such as *Red Sun* and some of the many Mount Fuji views he made. There are 100 works including pocketbook sketches, rare illustrations and detailed exhibits exploring the print-making process. Hokusai spent most of his life in the Sumida area, so the museum is a fitting tribute to his life and work.

KOISHIKAWA KORAKUEN
小石川後楽園

Koraku

1-6-6 Koraku, Bunkyo-ku

Mon–Sun 9am–5pm

‣ Suidobashi station, west exit

tokyo-park.or.jp/park/koishikawakorakuen

Finding tranquillity in a fast-paced city like Tokyo can be challenging, but we find that Koishikawa Korakuen garden offers a peaceful escape right in the heart of the metropolis. Easily accessible, this serene haven feels like a journey far from the urban hustle. A treasured gem from the Edo period and one of the last remaining 'daimyo' feudal lord gardens, Koishikawa Korakuen sits gracefully next to bustling Tokyo Dome City. Despite its peaceful atmosphere, you can hear rumbles and screams from the Thunder Dolphin roller-coaster, a surprising reminder that you are still within Tokyo's energetic bounds. True to the tradition of landscape gardens, it beautifully blends natural and built elements to create a series of famed Chinese and Japanese scenes that can be viewed from different angles. Our favourite thing in the garden, and to us a Tokyo highlight, is the stone 'full moon' bridge, which arches over a lake, forming a perfect circle in its reflection – it's a design inspired by Confucian scholar Shu Shunsui. Another iconic sight is the vermilion **Tsutenkyo Bridge**, a striking wooden structure that's a photographer's dream. The garden is particularly captivating in late November and early December, when its autumn foliage is in full display, though cherry blossoms in late March are another major attraction.

HISTORY NOTE

The **Tokyo National Museum** and the **Ota Museum** both have good collections of ukiyo-e prints.

ONSEN NOTE

Spa LaQua *(see p. 160)* is located in Tokyo Dome City, next to the gardens. Why not have a relaxing soak after your tranquil stroll?

EDO-TOKYO OPEN AIR ARCHITECTURAL MUSEUM
江戸東京たてもの園

Koganei

3-7-1 Sakuracho, Koganei-shi

Tues–Sun 9.30am–4.30pm

‣ Musashi-Koganei station, north exit

tatemonoen.jp

Slip back in time to when art and culture thrived and busy merchants linked the rural farming community with the developing city. Residing in Koganei park, this museum houses over 30 buildings, lovingly restored or re-created, making for an immersive experience that brings old Edo back to life. Opening in 1993, the museum's standout Edo moments include Tsunashima-ke, an original thatched roof farmer's house as well as the original House of the Leader of the Hachioji Guards. The grounds also feature a re-creation of a downtown Yamanote townscape, with an impressive teahouse and one of the museum's best exhibits, Kodakara-yu, a traditional bathhouse, where you can get up close and personal with a classic sento while keeping your clothes on. The bathhouse features a giant, detailed mural of Mount Fuji. Probably one of the main reasons many people visit the open-air museum is because it was a favourite haunt of Ghibli master animator Hayao Miyazaki, who was inspired by many of the buildings, most notably the bathhouse was used as one of the templates for the bathhouse in *Spirited Away*. It should be noted that many of the exhibits are actually from the Meiji period (1868–1912) or Showa period (1926–89), however the contrast of these with the Edo buildings serve as a notable example of how fast Tokyo society was developing in the 20th century.

HISTORY NOTE

The **Edo-Tokyo Museum** in Sumida (slated for reopening in 2026 after extensive renovations) features exhibits of Edo living.

NEZU SHRINE
根津神社

Nezu

1-28-9 Nezu, Bunkyo-ku

Mon–Sun 6am–6pm (garden), Mon–Sun 9.30am–5.30pm (temple)

› Nezu station, exit 1

nedujinja.or.jp

Dating to a staggering 1705, the early-to-mid Edo period Nezu shrine is history scented by flowers. A break from the city's frenetic pace, this hidden cultural gem provides welcome respite and a cleansing of the spirit. Home of the god of the sea and storms, Susanoo-no-Mikoto, the shrine's main structures are historically intact, a rarity for a city decimated by war and earthquakes over the centuries. Let the kitsune (fox) statues, messengers of the god Inari, help guide you on a contemplative walk through the temple grounds. Wind your way through the multitude of small vermilion torii gates (Senbon Torii) which are punctuated by a viewing platform overlooking an expansive pond filled with contented koi. Spring in Japan may be known for cherry blossoms, however come April, the shrine's **Tsutsuji Matsuri** (Azalea Festival) is one of the city's prettiest and most dramatic flower moments. The contemplative clientele turns joyous, making way for festive blooms and pop-up street food stalls, the shrine's bright red torii gates overlooking 3000 colourful azaleas in pink, red, purple and white.

HISTORY NOTE

Tranquil **Joshin-ji temple** (2 Chome-17-4 Mukogaoka) is only a 6min walk from Nezu shrine.

KAGURAZAKA
神楽坂

Shinjuku-ku

▸ Iidabashi station, exit B3

Resting on the lip of the outer grounds of the once-proud **Edo Castle**, Kagurazaka is a relaxed town where the ghosts of old Edo gently haunt the streets and lanes. A famed entertainment district, Kagurazaka was known for its geisha culture which dates back to 1788. Geisha activity reached its peak in 1937, and around 20 geisha still operate in Kagurazaka today. Several original geisha houses still stand as Kagurazaka was the only one of the 'Tokyo Rokkagai' (six geisha districts) that survived the Great Kanto earthquake of 1923. The best place to feel like you are living in that time is **Geisha Shindo** (Iidabashi station, exit B4b). **Akagi** shrine (Kagurazaka station, exit 1a) dates to around 1700, a classic example of an Edo period shrine, now embellished by a cutting-edge Kengo Kuma architectural addition. There are also two Edo period yokocho (old-world alleys with small eateries), **Kakurenbo** – 'Hide and Seek Alley' – and **Hyogo Yokocho** (both Iidabashi station, exit B4b). **Kagurazaka-dori** is a shopping strip with contemporary restaurants and stores, many of which have a French theme, giving the area its current nickname of 'Little Paris'. Picturesque eateries feature canal views with seasonal cherry blossoms.

KABUKI-ZA
歌舞伎座

Ginza

4-12-15 Ginza, Chuo-ku

▸ Higashi-Ginza station, exit 3

kabukiweb.net

Tragedy! Betrayal! Murder! Kabuki has it all. And we haven't even started on the hair, make-up, costumes and elaborate sets. The invention of kabuki harks back to the Edo period and it has history woven into its very fabric. It's atmospheric, moving and immersive, but you don't have to take in a show to experience kabuki. Head to Kabuki-za, originally built in 1889, but now refreshed with a 2013 facelift by Kengo Kuma. Features include a vibrant façade, rooftop garden, museum and teashop. The rough and tumble market in the basement, which is connected to Higashi-Ginza station, sells bento boxes and omiyage (regional souvenirs) bearing the trademark kabuki coloured stripes. Chances are once you are there, the allure of the art will inspire you to experience kabuki, and you can do so in segments, taking in some of the show with knowledge of the surrounding story, or you can settle in for the long haul. Either way, you can be sure that the Edo period will be brought dramatically to life!

AREA NOTE

Don't miss Monzen-Nakacho, a local neighbourhood where you'll find cobbled streets and long-standing stores. Visit at night for a lively Old Edo atmosphere. It's just just seven stations away from Kagurazaka on the Tozai line.

EDO-YU
江戸遊

Ryogoku

1-5-8 Kamezawa, Sumida-ku

Mon–Sun 24hr (except when closed for cleaning: 8.30–10am)

‣ Ryogoku station, exit A3 or A4

edoyu.com/ryougoku

Now it's time to step into the floating world of the Edo period where relaxation is taken to the next level and where you will be revived and inspired and bathing like it's 1699. Sitting proudly on Hokusai-dori, the super-sento Edo-yu is making waves as Tokyo's most stylish experiential bathhouse. Set over five floors, Edo-yu features baths, saunas, relaxing zones, separate floors for men and women and two eating spaces. Admire the spectacular frontage designed by Kubo Tsushima Architects, the large patterned exterior canopies are reminiscent of billowing bathhouse noren (traditional curtains), whilst also echoing the work of Sumida native woodblock master Hokusai. Lovers of interiors will note the tiles used, fabric choices and the walls of the baths decorated with murals depicting scenes of old Edo and re-creations of the classic Hokusai work, *Red Fuji* (Fine Wind, Clear Morning). Sex-segregated bathing experiences include a Chinese herbal medicine bath, a super jet bath, a high-concentration carbonated spring bath, three saunas, bedrock baths, and bookable experiences (massage, acupuncture and body maintenance and head care).

YANAKA CEMETERY
谷中霊園

Yanaka

7-5-24 Yanaka, Taito-ku

Mon–Sun 8.30am–5.15pm

‣ Nippori station, north exit

tokyo-park.or.jp/reien/yanaka

Originally known as Yanaka Bochi (graveyard), this mystical place is now called Yanaka Cemetery or Yanaka Spirit Park, a verdant expanse featuring notable graves, especially of authors and politicians, and a range of spectacular plantings. Though it opened a few years after the Edo period, it is significant because it is home to the remains of 15 Tokugawa Edo period shoguns, including the last shogun, Tokugawa Yoshinobu. At dusk, Yanaka's resident cats slink among the gravestones and the setting sun gives it a haunting stillness. Its infamous history includes a five-tiered pagoda, burnt down in an arson/double-suicide case from the 1950s that featured in an infamous novel by Koda Rohan. At the entrance is the enchanting Meiji period (1868–1912) flower shop, **Hanaju**, which dates back to 1870 and sells flowers and small brooms for sweeping graves clean. The autumn colours and cherry blossoms in season make the cemetery resplendent and if you are here during the final moments of hanami (cherry blossom season), the pink blossoms drift down and blanket the graves (known as sakura snow). The cemetery is even more haunting (and moving) during **Obon**, the festival of the dead, on 15 July, when families call out to the souls of their departed loved ones.

TRAVELLER'S NOTE

With hourly rates, day rates, a discount for groups of three and over (and a middle-aged discount) and an overnight surcharge, Edo-yu is the full experience with chic décor, amazing amenities and a reasonable price considering what's on offer.

TRAVEL TIPS
東京旅行のヒント

GETTING TO TOKYO
東京へのアクセス

Before you leave

To save you time at the airport, you can fill out the immigration form online (services.digital.go.jp/en/visit-japan-web).

Tokyo has two international airports: Narita and Haneda. Below is information about transport from the airports to the city.

From (and to) Narita

Narita Airport is 71km from the city. For all current public transport prices and routes, check ahead online (narita-airport.jp/en/access). Options include:

- The **Narita Express** train (jreast.co.jp/e/nex) which goes from Narita to Tokyo Station in 53min. After Tokyo, stops also include Shinagawa, Shibuya and Shinjuku and a separate route from Shinagawa even takes you to Yokohama. Buy a return ticket if you are coming back within a two-week period as they are discounted.
- The **Keisei Skyliner** train (keisei.co.jp) will take you to Nippori or Ueno stations in around 41min, handy if you are staying near these areas, or near Asakusa. You can transfer to the Yamanote line at Nippori or Ueno; this can get you to Tokyo Station in 10min. The Skyliner runs from 7.23am to 11.48pm.
- The **Keisei Limited Express** train is a rapid express (keisei.co.jp) and will get you to Ueno in 71min. If you are on a budget, and patient, this could be a good option. It operates from 5.41am to 10.30pm.
- The **Tokyo Shuttle** bus (keiseibus.co.jp) from Tokyo and Ginza stations is a slower but cheaper way to get to Narita Airport than trains. It takes around 65 to 75min and there is one every 20min.
- The **Limousine Bus** (limousinebus.co.jp/en) takes around 80 to 100min between Narita Airport and Tokyo (buses have stops all over Tokyo).
- **Taxis** from Narita Airport to the city are very expensive. They take 60 to 80min, depending on the traffic, however there are some great shared taxi services that can work out cheaper and shared car ride services. Shop around. Very handy if you have a lot of luggage.

From (and to) Haneda

Haneda Airport is 22km from the city. For all current public transport prices and routes, check ahead (haneda-airport.jp). Options include:

- The **Tokyo Monorail** (tokyo-monorail.co.jp/english) goes from Haneda to Hamamatsucho/Shinagawa station in 13min. You can also take the Keikyu line which gets you to Shinagawa station in 20min. Trains run between 9am and 5pm.
- The **Limousine Bus** (limousinebus.co.jp/en) takes around 35 to 75min to Shinjuku and as a bonus runs between midnight and 5am. There can be delays, depending on traffic conditions.
- **Taxis** are a more expensive option but are affordable from Haneda compared to Narita and much more convenient.
- **Limousine and shuttle services** can be budget-friendly if they have a specific deal. Ask at your hotel or head online (airportlimo-tokyo.com or tokyo-taxi.jp/english/service/index.html).

Luggage services

It's convenient, easy and affordable to send your luggage on to either airport. Not worrying about heavy bags or lugging them onto the train to the airport on your last day of travel makes things much breezier. Try **Airporter** (about.airporter.co.jp) or **Yamato Couriers** (kuronekoyamato.co.jp); yes, they're the ones with the cute black-and-yellow logo of the mother cat carrying her baby kitten.

GETTING AROUND TOKYO
東京での移動方法

Trains

Purchase a **Suica** or **Pasmo** card from machines at train stations. For a deposit of around ¥500, these cards are rechargeable and easy to use. Top them up at the machines (they have English instructions) and swipe them at the barrier gates to get into a station. You can also use them on buses, in station lockers, and in an increasing number of vending machines, restaurants and convenience stores. You can download the app and put the card on your phone, which is an easy way to load money on and a convenient option to tap on and off at ticket gates (jreast.co.jp/multi/en/wsmlp).

Train passes

Your main train lines in Tokyo will be the Yamanote and the Tokyo Metro network. Both can be paid for using the Suica or Pasmo, which can also be used on Tokyo's buses (*see* p. 213). However, there are day passes for train travel that are better value than paying each time you get on. A Japan Rail (JR) day pass can only be used on JR lines like the Yamanote line and a Metro Pass can only be used on the Tokyo Metro so get to know your train lines (our book *Train Japan*, published by Hardie Grant, helps a lot with this). You can always get a day pass on, say the Metro line and use your Suica or Pasmo to ride on the other lines when needed.

The **Yamanote line** is a central loop line, run by JR (you can use up any free days you have on the JR Pass, hooray!) that stops at many of the city's unmissable destinations like Tokyo Station, Ueno, Shibuya, Shinjuku, Ebisu and Harajuku. It includes a few surprising ones too (for example, Takadanobaba is the home of Astro Boy, and, as such, plays the *Astro Boy* theme as its station music). Always make sure you are heading in the right direction – or you will be completing the whole circle to get to your destination. You can use Suica/Pasmo but you can't use the Metro Pass on the Yamanote line. In winter the trains are warm, in summer, cool. Make a day of it! Ride the Yamanote and get off at random stations; you'll find all kinds of cool things.

Apart from the Yamanote loop line, the other main line is the **Tokyo Metro**. The tourist-only 24-, 48- and 72-hour **Metro Passes** are excellent value for sightseeing, even if you are only in Tokyo for just one day. Hopping on and off subway trains on the extensive Metro network is both a cost-effective and convenient way to travel around the city. The fixed, low price point means that if you travel on the Tokyo Metro many times in one day, savings can be significant. Note that stations can appear on both the Yamanote line and the Metro line, depending on which lines criss-cross at stations, so if planned properly, you can end up using the pass for most journeys. Metro tickets cannot be used on Japan Rail trains including the JR Yamanote line, JR lines or other private lines so make sure you have a Suica/Pasmo or valid JR Pass for those. You can purchase Metro Passes online (tokyometro.jp/en/ticket). Specific machines are available to scan the QR code you'll be given for your ticket. Only a few manned station outlets are available so pre-bought online cards are more convenient. You can also purchase the ticket at travel sites like Klook or H.I.S.

The Tokyo Metropolitan District Pass: **JR Tokunai Pass** is a well-priced one-day pass for unlimited rides on JR trains in central Tokyo. Search online for the stations it covers. Other passes you can buy in Tokyo include: Toden one-day pass (Arakawa line), Triangle ticket (Tokyu Railway), Setagaya Sansaku ticket (Tokyu Railway) and the Keio Inokashira line one-day pass (Inokashira line).

Multi-day train passes

There are two options for multi-day train passes which can be handy for daytrips outside of the city.

The **Greater Tokyo Pass** (greater-tokyo-pass.jp) is a five-day pass that you can use around the city on trains and buses (but not on JR lines) and also for Toei buses around Kanto, for instance you can go to popular daytrip destinations like Enoshima, Nikko and Mount Takao.

The **JR Tokyo Wide Pass** (jreast.co.jp/e/tokyowidepass) is a three-day pass that is for use on JR lines, and takes you to places like Nikko, Mount Fuji, and Izu.

Japan Rail seven- and 14-day passes (japanrailpass.net/en) are the main passes to travel on the shinkansen (bullet train) around Japan. They may also be perfect if you are planning on doing quite a few daytrips from Tokyo, as they will take you further and give you more scope than other passes.

If you're not keen on using the trains, the **Shinjuku Bus Terminal** offers lots of daytrips. Check the schedules and routes online (highway-buses.jp/terminal/shinjuku.php).

Train tips

- Know your station exit! It is easy to get lost.
- Trains run from around 5am to midnight.
- Trains have women-only cars at certain times, and some seats are reserved for the elderly, injured or pregnant. If you are pregnant, you can get a 'maternity badge' at train stations to make other travellers aware and mindful.
- Line up for the trains in designated areas and wait for all other passengers to get off before boarding. Cram yourself in at peak times; a Tokyo rush hour train cram is a rite of passage.
- If you have a train ticket but you're not sure whether it has enough value on it for your journey, you can adjust your fare at a fare-adjustment machine when you get to your destination.
- Trains are great fun, comfortable and often have little TVs playing very cute advertisements to help you pass the time.

Taxis

Taxis cost a set low rate for the first 1.052 kilometres, then add a fee for every kilometre after that. Late at night, fares can rise by 20 per cent. All tolls will be calculated in the cost of your fare.

You can sign up to GO, Japan's number one taxi app, for seamless connections across Tokyo. And always check to see if your preferred rideshare app is supported and cost effective.

Bikes

Riding a bike is a great way to get around a single neighbourhood. You can hire bikes at many places, including **Tokyo Bike** (*see* p. 146). You can also hire electric bikes (tokyo-rental-bicycle.com). **Docomo** (docomo-cycle.jp/Tokyo) run a popular bike share service.

Buses

Buses within Tokyo's 23 wards are to be entered from the front. Prices are fixed, so put your money (exact change) into the box next to the driver, get a ticket and exit from the rear. If you have a Suica or Pasmo card, it's easiest to swipe it on entry at the front of the bus, then leave at the back. The **Toei Bus One Day Pass** (kotsu.metro.tokyo.jp/eng/tickets) can be a good option if you plan a day of travel on buses in Tokyo's 23 wards.

Walking

You'll do a lot of walking in Tokyo – it's how you'll stumble across some of your best finds, so wear a good pair of shoes!

At major crossings, when the pedestrian light turns green, all traffic stops and people go in all directions! It's called 'the scramble' and Shibuya's crossing is the famous one. Join in the fun: when the lights change, launch yourself into the chaos. It's estimated that about 1000 people cross at Shibuya at any one time!

Navigating

A map app is your friend in Tokyo. Once you've found the right train station exit, look on your map app for identifiable places, like convenience stores, museums or banks, and get your bearings from there. You can also ask at police boxes, or ask a local: they may not speak English but it's likely they'll walk you to your destination no matter how far out of their way they have to go.

Shopping

When you enter a shop (or restaurant), staff will say 'irasshaimase', which means 'you are welcome'. There's not really an answer to this, but sometimes it's so emphatic you'll feel like saying something in return! Just say 'konnichiwa' (hello). Shopping in Tokyo is extensive and ranges from huge superstores to small local maker stores. Always be polite. Ask before you try something on. Bags will usually cost extra so always bring your own. Browsing is encouraged. (*see* Tokyo Shopping chapter p. 20)

Tax

There is a 10 per cent consumption tax in Japan. This is sometimes included in the listed price, but often isn't, so check first. Sometimes a 'service charge' is added – for hotels and restaurants this can really stack up. Make sure you're aware of any additional costs before making a purchase.

Tax free

As of 2026, tax-free refunds will be done at the airport entirely to stop the resale of tax-free goods within Japan. Purchases eligible for tax free will be noted in your passport and refunds given at the airport tax-free counter.

Manners

Manners are very important in Japan, so always be as polite as possible. Invoke your inner sense of calm and treat everyone with respect, and respect will be returned to you. The deeper someone bows, the more respect they are showing you. Most younger people don't bow as much now, but a slight bow of the head is always a good thing.

Take off your shoes before walking onto a tatami mat or entering a house. A lot of restaurants also require you to remove your shoes, but the staff will let you know. You should take your shoes off when entering a clothing store changing room.

Don't take photographs of people or in shops without asking first.

Japanese people are considerate of each other's space and don't speak loudly whilst on board trains, or use earbuds or headphones when on their phone. Phone use on trains is prevalent, but is strictly visual – no one has their phone sound enabled or talks on their phone, and neither should you. Eating or drinking on board local trains is not good manners, either.

If you're sick with a cold, wear a face mask everywhere.

Also, don't take a wet umbrella into a shop; use the bags or holders provided. You can ask your hotel for an umbrella, buy a good quality small umbrella from Muji or Loft, or hire an umbrella from a train station for the day.

Onsen and sento etiquette

There are set rules and a conduct code at sento (bathhouse) and onsen (hot springs) that can be a little daunting but you get used to them quickly and they are mostly based on manners. Tattoos may or may not be allowed in onsen, so always ask first; many local sento will allow them, but bigger onsen are likely not to. There will usually be a 'how to' guide in English so study it carefully, or look up online before you go. Feel free to pick up our book, *Onsen of Japan*, published by Hardie Grant, for more info!

Crime

Crime is low in Tokyo. There are very few dangerous areas. Honestly, you could drop your wallet and someone will pick it up and give it back to you, or if you left it somewhere, it will likely be mailed to you or taken to the nearest koban (police box).

Toilets

Public toilets are easy to find and range from the basic to the so-intricate that you'll never have time to work out all of the functions. Some toilets play music, so pick a tune! The nicest toilets are located in department stores. Some public toilets are squat ones, so beware, or dare! If you're interested in designer toilets, see The Tokyo Toilet project (*see* p. 178).

Addresses

Even Tokyo-ites have trouble with the city's address system – they use map apps as well! Always consult a map app, and navigate using nearby landmarks, shrines or convenience stores. A typical Tokyo address will read like this: 5-35-1 Daita Setagaya. In order, the numbers stand for subsection (ward), block number and then building number. In Tokyo, the ground floor is referred to as the first floor (1F; the next floor up is 2F), and the floor beneath that is the basement. There's no point looking for street names as most streets don't have names! The ones that do were mostly named by the Americans after World War II to help them get around.

Convenience stores

Tokyo's convenience stores, or konbini, are awesome. You might be used to convenience stores having higher prices for junky products, but in Tokyo they are fast, cheap, convenient and sell great stuff, including cheap beer, fresh fruit and vegetables, sweets, magazines and delicious takeaway food. Sometimes they have their own select ranges, and **FamilyMart** stocks Muji products. You can also buy concert and museum tickets. We could happily do a convenience store tour of Tokyo. FamilyMart, **Lawson** and **7-Eleven** are the main stores, but look out for cute neighbourhood versions too as well as luxe versions like FamilyMart's **Famima** and Lawson's **Natural Lawson**.

Vending machines

Vending machines are everywhere. The variety of drinks they have is staggering – convenient if you want a hot green tea or coffee in winter or cold drink at any time of the year. They can also sell anything from hamburgers to toilet paper, stationery, shirts, alcohol and cup noodles.

Money

Japan's currency is the yen, denoted by ¥. It comes in denominations of ¥1000, ¥2000, ¥5000, and ¥10,000 in notes, and ¥1, ¥5, ¥10, ¥50, ¥100 and ¥500 in coins. The ¥5 and ¥50 coins have holes in the middle of them.

Not all ATMs take international cards, so if you need to get cash, try a **Seven Bank**. International ATMs can also be found in some large stores and department stores, 7-Eleven stores, some konbini (convenience stores) and in most post offices.

Many small towns are still cash-based and you can be hard pressed to find an ATM or exchange money. So be prepared and have enough cash on you in advance.

Very large 'hub' stations have money exchange counters, and all large stations have a post office which can give you better rates when exchanging money.

Electronics

Tokyo has great electronic gadgets and devices, but remember to check that wattage and plugs are compatible to your home country. If you really have to buy something, you'll need to get it converted or buy a transformer device. Some stores will sell Western versions, which have already been changed over. Duty-free places at the airport may sell products with Western-style wattage.

Phones & wi-fi

To access wi-fi in Tokyo, you have a few options. Many travellers rent pocket wi-fi at Narita Airport or Bic Camera to use with their smartphone. You can also hire a mobile phone at the airport, or buy a SIM card for your phone; at outlets around the city such as SoftBank or Docomo, Tokyo's major mobile phone providers. 7-Eleven stores sell sims and also have free wi-fi you can log onto, as do Loft stores, and on the Yamanote train line and Tokyo Metro. Information at Hikarie ShinQs (*see* p. 37) will set you up with 'Visit Shibuya', a week of free wi-fi for Shibuya hotspots (you'll need your passport).

Some hotels now provide pocket wi-fi or a smartphone in the room so remember to ask before you book, as it may make a difference to your choice.

If you search for pocket wi-fi online you'll see the myriad of choices, many have cheaper deals if you book online. Try: pocket-wifi-japan.com, rentalwifi.com,japan-wireless.com, or japan-experience.com/internet-access/pocket-wifi.

Prepaid mobile SIM card

SIM cards can be bought in your home country. Check rates with your provider before you leave for Japan to see if they are competitive. Although it certainly wasn't once the case, quite often these days it is cheaper and easier to use your mobile with roaming data. Alternatively, you can buy a SIM card at electronics stores and convenience stores in Tokyo. It is also easy to buy them at the airport or at 7-Eleven. Ask at Information for directions or look out for b-Mobile, SoftBank, Mobal, eSIM, Global WiFi and Ninja WiFi. J Walker SIM have convenient automatic sales machines.

Chargers for your phone can be found in convenience stores, stations, and shopping centres, rented for the day for small change, and then returned (note the brand so you can return it to the right machine). Available brands include ChargeSpot, Juren and HESTA CHARGE.

EATING OUT KNOW-HOW
外食のヒントとマナー

- Make sure you check the opening hours of your desired cafe or restaurant.
- Most cafes and bars shut for one day during the week, and many cafes open around 11am.
- If you don't speak Japanese, ask your hotel to make restaurant reservations on your behalf (they may decline to do this).
- Lunch starts at 11.30am and finishes between 2 and 3pm. Set lunches are great value, especially at places that do an expensive dinner.
- It's good fun to try the omakase (chef's choice) at restaurants. The chefs decide what they think is the best choice for you.
- Many small eateries have plastic food models out the front of their establishment, and many cafes have pictorial menus, which is very handy if you don't speak Japanese. You can show a staff member the menu, point to your preferred dish and say 'please': either 'onegaishimasu' (polite) or 'okudasai'.
- It is customary to pour other people's drinks.
- Most places are licensed.
- When using chopsticks, don't stick them upright in a bowl of rice – this is a funeral custom. Also, don't pass food to, or take food from, other people using chopsticks, and don't spear food with them (okay, we may have done this a few times ...). Lastly, don't use chopsticks to move a bowl towards you.
- If you want to eat with the salarymen and locals, there are many great, inexpensive options centred around or inside train stations.
- Make sure you try a kissaten. These retro coffee shops are a unique Japanese experience.
- Some smaller eateries will still only take cash.
- Tipping is not a thing in Tokyo. In fact, it will cause confusion.

Handy tip for vegetarians and vegans

If you are a vegetarian or vegan, come armed with the phrase 'Watashi wa niku o tabemasen' or 'I don't eat meat'. A shorthand is to make a cross with your hands and say the word niku (the word for meat) or the word for 'vegetarian' is 'bejitarian' and vegan is 'bee-gan'.

USEFUL WORDS & PHRASES 役立つ日本語フレーズ集

Japanese pronunciation is simply this: the five vowels are 'a' (pronounced like the 'u' in up), 'i' (pronounced like the 'i' in imp), 'u' (pronounced as the 'oo' in book), 'e' (pronounced as the 'e' in egg) and 'o' (pronounced as the 'o' in lock). This doesn't change for any word, and if two vowels are placed together, you say them as if they were separate vowel sounds in a row. Simple! The letter 'r' is pronounced as a cross between an 'r' and an 'l'; the easiest way to make this sound is to touch the roof of your mouth with the tip of your tongue. Japanese language uses three alphabets: Hiragana words use phonetic sounds and there are 46 alphabet characters such as ka, ki, ku, ke and ko. Hiragana is used for Japanese words, so even if you learn the alphabets, which is relatively easy, you need to have all the corresponding vocabulary. Kanji is derived from Chinese characters and has thousands of symbols to learn, each with both a Japanese and a Chinese reading and phonetic to match. A daunting task, but it can be relatively easy to learn a handful of them such as numbers (useful for older-style menus). Katakana is used for words such as brand names or food/menu items that derive from foreign words. The syllables are easy to learn and the pronunciations are essentially loan words so if you learn these, you'll find that you can read some signs and speak some Japanese in no time. For example; タ(ta)ク(ku)シ(shi) = Takushi = taxi. It's especially handy for reading menus as things like coffee and sandwiches are loan words anyway. Learning the hiragana for many types of food is relatively easy and will also greatly help you with menus.

Useful kanji

Learning the kanji for 'Tokyo' is useful for reading the weather on TV.

Tokyo: 東京

Male and female kanji is also useful for toilet signage.

Male: 男

Female: 女

Japan: 日本

Yen: 円

Enter: 入口

Exit: 出口

North: 北

South: 南

East: 東

West: 西

Do you speak English?: *anata wa eigo o hanashimasu ka?*

I don't understand: *wakarimasen*

I don't understand Japanese: *Nihongo ga wakarimasen*

Hello: *konnichiwa*

Good morning: *ohayou gozaimasu*

Goodnight: *oyasuminasai*

Goodbye: *sayonara*

See you later: *mata ne*

Nice to meet you: *hajimemashite*

Please: *kudasai/onegaishimasu*

Thank you: *arigato, arigato gozaimasu*

Thank you very much: *domo arigato*

Excuse me: *sumimasen*

How are you?: *genki desu ka?*

I'm well: *genki desu* or *genki*

How much is this?: *ikura desu ka?*

I'll take this: *kore o kaimasu*

Cheers!: *kanpai!*

I would like a beer please: *biru wo kudasai* (or add *nama* before *biru* for a draught beer)

Delicious: *oishii*

Can I have the bill please?: *okanjo onegaishimasu?*

After eating a delicious meal say: *gochisousama deshita*

Train station: *eki*

Airport: *kuukou*

Taxi: *takushi*

I love Japan!: *watashi wa Nihon ga daisuki!*

RECOMMENDED HOTELS
おすすめのホテル

Accommodation in Tokyo comes in all shapes, sizes and styles. Rooms are usually small, but newer hotels are using the space more effectively. Note: some of the listings below may vary significantly in price depending on what season you are travelling in.

Capsules

The Millennials, Anshin Oyado, Book Tea Bed, Manga Art Hotel, 9 hours, Hotel Tomariya, Nadeshiko Hotel Shibuya (Female Only), First Cabin, Resol Poshtel.

Hostels

Nui. Hostel & Bar Lounge, UNPLAN Kagurazaka, Waves Nakameguro, Grids, &AND HOSTEL ASAKUSA KAPPABASHI.

Well-known brands

Dormy Inn, Remm, Mitsui Garden, The b Group.

Well priced & stylish

Omo Hotels, Hotel Graphy, Granbell Hotels, Hotel Hillarys Akasaka, One@Tokyo, Hotel Gajoen Tokyo, DDD Hotel.

Boutique

Trunk Hotel, Park Hotel, Muji Hotel, Nogha Hotel, 1899 Hotel, Mustard Hotel Shimokitazawa, Agora Hotel Ginza.

Luxe

Tokyo Station Hotel, Andaz Hotel, Kimpton Shinjuku Tokyo, Hotel K5.

Stylish 20th-century hotels

Hotel Okura, Hotel Chinzanso, Sheraton Miyako Hotel.

Ryokan (traditional Japanese inns)

Onsen Ryokan Yuen Shinjuku, Ryokan Asakusa Shigetsu, Kimi Ryokan, Takemine, Andon Ryokan, Kaminarimon Ryokan, Sakura Ryokan Asakusa Iriya, Hotel Fukudaya.

Out-of-this-world ryokan experiences

Hoshinoya Tokyo.

HOLIDAYS & SEASONS
日本の祝日と四季

Public holidays & festivals

There are 16 public holidays in Japan each year, all celebrated in Tokyo, including Children's Day, Respect For The Aged Day, Marine Day and Shichi-Go-San (meaning: 7-5-3) where the health and wellbeing of children of these ages is celebrated. Check your holiday dates against a list online, as businesses may be closed or crowded, especially during Golden Week which usually starts on one of the last days of April and extends into the first week of May. Hanami (cherry blossom season) will also be busy. Book your accommodation and train travel well in advance if you will be in Tokyo at these times.

Christmas Day is a normal working day in Tokyo. Christmas Eve is considered 'date night' in Japan, especially for the young. New Year is the big holiday in Japan. Celebrations involve visits to Shinto shrines to pray for good fortune and health in the coming year. Special wreaths called Shimekazari are hung on doors. A tradition going back 400 years, they are made of rice straw and placed on doors for good luck and to welcome deities. Businesses can close the week before New Year, and stay shut for the first few weeks of January. Check attractions before you visit.

Seasons

Spring's famous sakura (cherry blossoms) arrive in Japan anywhere from the last week of March until the first week of April. Blossoms typically last a week.

Autumn foliage is sublime in Tokyo with leaves starting to turn in mid-November, peaking in the last week of November, and finally succumbing to winter in mid-December.

Crisp winter days with clear blue skies make for perfect woolly weather to sightsee or cosy up in a cafe with a cup of matcha and zenzai (sweet soupy dessert). The cold sets in from December to February.

Summer in Japan is very hot and humid. Dress light and carry cooling aids and small sweat-soaking towels (found in most convenience stores). Try to stay in hotels that have air conditioning or visit shopping centres and museums that are cooled. Months to stay cool are June, July and August. Rainy season typically starts in the first week of June.

INDEX
索引

ABOUT THE AUTHORS
著者について

Steve Wide and **Michelle Mackintosh** have been obsessed with Japan since their first visit in the late 1990s. They now call Japan their 'home away from home', spending at least three months of the year there.

Steve is a writer and DJ who hosts a long-standing indie radio show on 3RRRFM. He has interviewed, DJ-ed and toured with international bands, hosted clubs and written 10 pop-culture books on music icons. He's also written six quirky books for children.

Michelle is an award-winning book designer and illustrator who has written three books on analogue correspondence and sustainable gifting, and *Pretend You're in Tokyo (*Harper By Design, 2022), an armchair travel book on how to bring Japan into your daily life. She has contributed to panel discussions and podcasts on the role of design in Japanese culture and the art and craft of book design. Her work has been exhibited in Tokyo.

Together Steve and Michelle have written, designed, photographed and illustrated ten books on Japan: The following were published by Hardie Grant Explore: *Tokyo Precincts* (2015), *Kyoto Pocket Precincts* (2017), *Onsen of Japan* (2018), *Tokyo Pocket Precincts* (2019), *Osaka Pocket Precincts* (2020), *Mindfulness Travel Japan* (2022), *Hidden Pockets in Kyoto* (2024) and *Train Japan* (2024). These books were published by Plum Books: *Tokyo* (2018) and *Japan* (2022). Steve and Michelle also co-wrote the Dorling Kindersley (DK) book *Be More Japan* (2019). Their books have been translated into multiple languages.

Michelle and Steve live in Melbourne/Naarm with their British shorthair cat Enid.

THANK YOU
ありがとう

We're endlessly grateful to all those who helped us ink the pages of this sprawling Historical Romance.

To Amanda Louey and Alice Barker who, like fearless Shibuya traffic cops, kept this whole project from turning into a chaotic scramble. Thanks to Tahlia Anderson who made sure we didn't get lost down any sketchy Kabukicho alleyways, and to Cassie Holland for ensuring our iced-matchas had the perfect dollop of ice-cream on top. Thank you to our Hardie Grant Explore crew past and present, Roxy, Lauren and Megan, Melissa and Danielle for helping pick the ripest yuzu. To the unstoppable Megan Ellis, our Ginza lunching lady who arranged the text on every page until it shone brighter than a neon sign. To our talented and bilingual friend Hikaru Komura, as precious as a golden koi in the lakes of Rikugien gardens.

To our treasured Japanese friends, Hiki, Ryo, Coco, Makiko, Shoko and Midori and to those dear to us who accompanied us on this journey, in person or in spirit. To our Hello Kitty Crew, Maximum Bygraves, Rita Tushingham and May May, fellow craft-holics Tiffany and Kylie, and birthday trip besties Mel and Elida. And of course, eternal love and thanks to the Mackintosh and Wide families — our human equivalents of a cosy konbini on a late-night stroll.

To our fabulous online and reading community — thank you for trusting us to share Tokyo's wonder with you. Your support is a like a perfect sakura bloom in Ueno park.

In memory of Emma and Isaac Roberts, Max Dariol and Cheryll Johnson.

Published in 2026 by Hardie Grant Explore, an imprint of Hardie Grant Publishing

Hardie Grant Explore (Melbourne)
Wurundjeri Country
Level 11, 36 Wellington Street
Collingwood, Victoria 3066

Hardie Grant Explore (Sydney)
Gadigal Country
Level 7, 45 Jones Street
Ultimo, NSW 2007

hardiegrant.com/explore

NATIONAL LIBRARY OF AUSTRALIA

A catalogue record for this book is available from the National Library of Australia

Hardie Grant acknowledges the Traditional Owners of the Country on which we work, the Wurundjeri People of the Kulin Nation and the Gadigal People of the Eora Nation, and recognises their continuing connection to the land, waters and culture. We pay our respects to their Elders past and present.

For all relevant publications, Hardie Grant Explore commissions a First Nations consultant to review relevant content and provide feedback to ensure suitable language and information is included in the final book. Hardie Grant Explore also includes traditional place names and acknowledges Traditional Owners, where possible, in both the text and mapping for their publications.

Tokyo Story
ISBN 9781741179477

10 9 8 7 6 5 4 3 2 1

Publisher
Tahlia Anderson

Project Editor
Amanda Louey

Editor
Alice Barker

Proofreader
Cassie Holland

Design & illustration
Michelle Mackintosh

Typesetting
Megan Ellis

Index
Max McMaster

Production Manager
Simone Wall

Colour reproduction by Megan Ellis and Splitting Image Colour Studio

Printed in China by LEO Paper Products LTD.

FSC www.fsc.org MIX Paper | Supporting responsible forestry FSC® C020056

The paper this book is printed on is from FSC®-certified forests and other controlled sources. FSC® promotes environmentally responsible, socially beneficial and economically viable management of the world's forests.

Image credits

All images are copyright Steve Wide and Michelle Mackintosh except the following.

pp. 2–3 © Maenohara Onsen Sayano Yudokoro; p. 7 bottom © Hikaru Komura; pp. 8–9 © Ippodo; p. 11 top © Higashiya; p. 13 top © Tokoan, Imperial Palace Hotel; pp. 14–15 © Kungyokudo; p. 25 © Moonstar; p. 47 top © Galerie Doux Dimanche; p. 52 bottom © Itoya; p. 55 top © Kylie and Tiffany Johnson; p. 59 © SuRyo; p. 143 © minä perhonen; p. 163 © Markus Spiske Unsplash; p. 175 © Susann Schuster Unsplash; p. 183 © Nakaharu Line Unsplash; p. 226 © Tina Bouhoutsos.